HIDDEN STRENGTH
LOVE, LOSS AND RESILIENCE

Tracey McAtamney

HIDDEN STRENGTH - LOVE, LOSS AND RESILIENCE

ISBN: 978-1-5272-3482-6

First published in Great Britain
in 2018 through Amazon self-publishing
service Kindle Direct Publishing

To protect the identities of parties that wish not to be named or identified: names and locations have been changed by the author.

Produced by samanthahoughton.co.uk

For Anthony & Oliver
In Loving Memory of Tony McAtamney, and for all those coping with bereavement.

Contents

HIDDEN STRENGTH

Acknowledgements

This book is for everyone coping with bereavement, it happens to us all.

Thank you to the special people in my life for their love and support. My Boys, Anthony and Oliver together with my step children, Helen, Victoria and Gerard, Daddy would have been so proud of you all! To Philip McIntyre for his love. To Lesley & Ray Allen, for always being there. My Sister Tina, for her constant support and my nieces, Natasha, Stephanie, Beth; and Nephew Tom. To Father Kevin Hooper and Father Frank Smith for their kindness and spiritual guidance together with the Parishioners of Blessed Robert Grissold. To Brian Sheridan, David Barker and the Law Society Golf Club. To Berkswell Church of England School. To my Accountants Mike Wilson, Marlene Hills and good friends Anne and Dominic O'Brien for their financial guidance. To Michael Hammon of Hammons Solicitors for his support in my time of need. To my wonderful friends for their unconditional friendship, Gill and Robin Peacock, Alison McDowall, Christina and Brian Richards, Karen and Paul Morris, Nikki Paton, Yvonne Cure, Gillian Stocks, Fiona and

Alex Ambrosioni, David McAtamney, Lorraine Baillie, Jenny and John Churchley. To my uncles Ben and Les and aunties Renee and Pat. To Tony Cotterill, for those many weekly visits checking the boys and I were okay, you certainly kept your promise. To the Saint Bernadette Trust & the O'Donnell family, my Lourdes family and the many lovely people I have met over the years, especially Adele Callinan. To Naomi O'Halloran, for looking after me after my accident and to Andrew Bonell and Jason Claridge for restoring my faith in Lawyers! To Susie Mackie and Pauline Edden, two truly inspirational ladies!

Phillip Townshend RIP and Steve Edmonds RIP.

Love and gratitude always to my wonderful Mum, Shirley Thomas RIP.

To everyone mentioned in my book and to those I may have missed out - I love you all.

Special, special thanks to Samantha Houghton for giving me the courage to write my story!

Prologue

I was born Tracey-Anne Lynch, daughter of Shirley and Tommy Lynch and younger sister to Tina Maria. When I was aged seven and my sister aged ten, our Dad died suddenly in a fall breaking his neck. We were raised by our amazing Mother, who protected us like a lioness caring for her cubs.

I left school at seventeen and started my first job in an Insurance Brokers, I also started a part time modelling career. At the age of nineteen I became Coventry Carnival Queen, Miss Coventry City, Miss Motoring Godiva and Miss Bedworth Echo. An exhausting year where I raised a lot of money for charity including jumping out of an airplane and launching the Coventry Evening Telegraph Snow Ball Appeal.

At the age of 22 I married Tony, he was the sole practitioner of a Solicitor's firm in Coventry which we ran together, my role being in charge of the accounts and general office management. Tony was divorced when I met him and the Father of three lovely children, Helen, Victoria and Gerard. We later had two sons Anthony and Oliver. We were happy!

Chapter 1
Don't Cry, Mummy

28th June 2004 - 29th June 2004

I sit bolt upright startled by the sudden shrill of my mobile phone ringing from the bedside table. I must have been in a deep sleep and as I glanced quickly at the small sleeping child next to me I am relieved he has not woken. I can hear the boys, Anthony my fifteen-year-old son and John his friend making noise in the next bedroom, still packing for their holiday the next day.

I snatch the still ringing phone and move as quickly as possible into the en suite bathroom and gently close the door. Who could be ringing at this time, it has to be past midnight?

As I press the answer button I hear a slight pause and then my name, 'Tracey', just my name and then a silence. I know the voice immediately, it is Brian Sheridan, one of my husband's golfing companions. Brian has a very distinctive soft voice, I don't know him that well but I recognise his voice.

I feel my stomach somersault and from nowhere I hear myself respond, 'He's dead, isn't he?' and as the soft voice responds, 'yes', I feel like I have been punched in the stomach.

As I urge myself to breathe, I drop to the floor before I fall down. 'Brian, can I call you back please, Ollie is sleeping in my bed and I do not want to wake him. He always sleeps with me when Tony is away'. I sound so calm and yet my whole body is shaking uncontrollably, this couldn't really be happening I tell myself, as Brian agrees to wait for my call.

With that I lift myself up and open the bathroom door, Oliver's eyes are shut tightly together and as he continues to sleep on, oblivious to what the morning is going to bring, I have never felt such despair in all my life. How am I going to tell my boys that their Daddy is not coming home?

As I stagger along the landing still struggling to breathe, Anthony's bedroom door opens. I hear him ask me what is wrong and I open my mouth to speak and at first no words will come out. Then the words are there, 'Daddy's dead', in the end there is no other way to say it. We stand clinging to each other for what seems like hours, but it isn't, it is just minutes. Minutes where my brave son does not cry, he just holds me tightly trying to stop me shaking.

Poor John, Anthony's lifelong school friend is ashen, he comes across and wraps his arms around us both, muttering words of 'so sorry'. I really want this to be a bad dream and pinch myself and reality suddenly starts to set in, this is real and happening.

I know I need to break the news to my Mum in the Granny Flat and then I need to call Brian in Spain to get the full story which of course I still don't know.

Just then, Oliver calls out to me. He has woken and has found me missing from the bed. Anthony and John immediately say that they will look after him until he goes back to sleep. Telling a seven-year-old child that his Daddy has died at 1.00 in the morning does not seem like a great plan, so I am relieved as I hear the boys telling him that everything is okay, Mummy just has a toothache.

I make my way into my Mum's Granny Flat. I tap the bedroom door in the hope that I will not make her jump and give her a heart attack, things are bad enough as it is. Mum sits up and looks at me, a look of worry is spreading across her face. As I break the news she begins to cry and shakes her head saying this cannot be happening. I am shocked, it is not what I had expected. Mum has always been so strong, I have rarely seen her cry. She is a great believer that you put your lip stick on, you get up and you smile, no matter how bad things are. Not this time, it is one shock too many for her and she crumbles.

Deep down I know the reason, my Dad had died in an accident when I was just seven and my sister ten. Mum had coped then. She was the strongest, most dignified person I had ever met and she protected her girls like a lioness protecting her cubs. It was all too much seeing this happen again but this time to her daughter and grandchildren. We hug and I find myself telling her that everything will be alright.

With trepidation I make the international call to Spain. Brian is waiting for my call. He sounds terribly sad. We speak for over thirty minutes, and I listen intently as he tells me that he had been told that Tony had felt unwell in the afternoon whilst playing golf. It was the first day of the competition and there had been a lot of excitement between the teams of golfers. Brian was playing with a different team at another Golf Club. Apparently, Tony had suddenly excused himself and returned to his room. Brian found out later that Tony had called a doctor who had gone to the room and examined him. He had been complaining about a back ache but had also seemed quite agitated. He must have thought there was a serious problem because Tony didn't make a fuss and rarely saw a doctor unless I insisted. Why hadn't he called me? I don't understand why, if he felt ill enough to call a doctor, why hadn't he called me to tell me he felt so ill?

I ask Brian why David Barker had not called me, David was Secretary of the Law Society Golf, I knew him well. I had spoken to David only last week, we had laughed and joked and he had promised to take care of Tony for me. Oh dear, I suddenly understand - he cannot face talking to me - surely he doesn't think that I would hold him responsible.

The Doctor had not found anything significant and had apparently left leaving some pain killers and muscle relaxants. It wasn't until after dinner that the other golfers had realised that Tony had not appeared for dinner. They tried calling his room but no answer. The Manager was called and the door opened. Tony was lying on the floor, he was dead.

I gasp with pain. I had presumed he had had a heart attack on the golf course and that he had died with people around him. I am mortified to discover he was all alone. I ask whether a priest had been called and Brian assures me that one had and had given Tony his last rites after death.

The golfers were waiting for Brian to return from the other golfing venue. Poor Brian, he had returned merry from a great day of golf and a jovial meal to find that he had been delegated to call and tell me the awful news. I begin to realise just how awful it must be for Tony's colleagues in Spain. I arrange to speak to Brian in the morning, I cannot take it all in. Brian tells me that whilst he has been talking to me, he has found himself standing in a fountain in the hotel grounds, he has been oblivious to the water and the fact he is soaked to the skin!

This feels like the longest darkest night of my life - it is still only 1.30am. I don't know what to do next. I know everyone is sleeping but I need to talk, I pick up the telephone and call our good friends Lesley and Ray Allen, it has only been two days since they had dropped Tony off with his golf clubs at a service station to meet Brian for the journey to Stanstead.

As I tell Lesley what has happened, I feel like I am having an outer body experience, this is nothing more than a bad dream I will wake up from very soon - but of course, it isn't. Within minutes cars are pulling up on the drive. Firstly, Father Kevin, a priest friend I have known since I was thirteen years old. Mum had called him immediately and he had driven straight over. Lesley and Ray pull up behind. There is an eerie silence on the drive as nobody really knows what to say, they put their arms around Anthony, Mum and I, nobody wants to wake Oliver.

Mum goes into making tea mode, we all gather in the lounge in complete shock. Anthony is incredibly brave. He and John also go into making tea mode and we all begin to pray for daylight. It is so unfair Anthony has finished his last GCSE yesterday. Today he should be flying out to Spain with John and his family to celebrate. I picture them both when they first met at Kindergarten, aged three and dressed in a bright purple school uniform with tie and cap. They became instant friends. Now standing next to me as young adults trying to deal with this awful situation, I suppose it could be worse, it could have happened whilst Anthony was away.

Father Kevin says some prayers with us all and then he discusses with me the decisions I will have to make quite quickly. Decisions like am I going to travel to Spain to see Tony, it will be the only opportunity I will have because of how bodies are preserved in Spain. These are things I really don't want to think about at the moment.

More friends arrive, as Robin Peacock comes through the front door, I announce that I need to get out and walk, I need to think, I need air. Robin takes my arm and we walk, we walk for over an hour. It is just starting to get light and the birds are beginning to sing. I had imagined daylight would ease the pain, but it hasn't. I still have to do the worst thing imaginable, I have to rock my little boy's world by telling him his Daddy has died!

Oliver adored his Daddy, he was his hero. His special day was always Saturday morning when he had Daddy time whilst I took Anthony to different classes and sports games. They had their own little routine of walking to the village and buying eggs from the Butcher, buying a newspaper and walking home - the whole time Ollie would talk non-stop to his Daddy, not even stopping for breath. He would ask every question imaginable whilst Tony was cooking breakfast- it was their time.

We make our way home and I brace myself for what has to be done.

The anguish on all the faces is obvious as they wait and watch as I make my way back upstairs to my bedroom. I can hear Oliver stirring. His little bright face is smiling as I walk into the room but it begins to change and I hear him say, 'You look sad Mummy'.

I climb into the bed and cuddle him for a moment. 'My darling, I have something sad that I have to tell you'. His reaction is instant, he holds his hands up and touches my eyes, his voice now frantic,' Mummy, don't cry, don't cry, Mummy'. I hadn't realised that I had tears in my eyes and I know immediately if the only thing I can do to ease Oliver's pain is not to cry, I will not cry.

As I promise not to cry a gentle smile spreads across my face, it hurts so much, but the smile is in place, I'm not sure it reaches my eyes, but I am not going to cry. I find myself explaining that Daddy has been taken to heaven. 'He hadn't wanted to leave us, but God had some very special work for him. Daddy will be by our side every day and every night. He will watch over us and keep us safe and if we look really hard at the night sky, he will be the brightest star in the sky.'

Oliver's face is quivering, but he is refusing to cry, I tell him it is okay to cry and it is okay to feel sad. I am holding my breath, I really don't know how he is going to react, my heart is breaking with every second. I kiss his face and hold his hands and ask him if there is anything he wants to ask me. After a few seconds he replies, 'Do I have to go to school today?' I let out a genuine laugh as I tell him that no, he wouldn't be going to school today. Next question, 'Can we go down stairs now?' I smile and lift him up into my arms to carry him downstairs, he suddenly whispers in my ear, 'Mummy, will you help me find the brightest star tonight?'

Chapter 2
The Previous Week

Like most families our day to day life is manic, this week is no exception and, in some ways, more manic than usual.

Tony is preparing for his trip to Spain, to Novo Sancti Petri in Cadiz for the 5th European Legal Team Championship with the Law Society Golf Club. He loves his golf trips. This one was different as we would usually all be travelling with him as a family. Anthony was due to take his final GCSE at Princethorpe College on the 28th June so I needed to be at home with him.

Monday morning comes and I drop Oliver off at school and continue my journey into the office in Coventry. Tony is a sole practitioner of a small but very busy Solicitors Office. I help manage the office and I am responsible for the legal accounts, basically taking care of the clients' money. We have a special treat today as we are collecting Helen, Tony's daughter from the station and we are going out to lunch. Helen lives in London with her husband Labi and although we do not see them as often as we would have liked, it is always lovely when we do.

Helen is glowing when we pick her up, I know this can only mean one thing. As we order lunch Helen calmly drops into the conversation that Tony will soon be a Grandad. He is speechless for once and utterly over the moon. Baby is due late December early January, it might even be born on Tony's birthday which is the 15th January! It is a happy and memorable lunch.

Tuesday arrives and although Tony is busy at the office, he always has time for his close friends and today is Tony Cotterill's birthday. Work in the morning is followed by a game of golf and I join them later in the evening with the other wives for a celebration dinner. Several of his dearest friends are present and it is an evening full of laughter.

Wednesday, I spend the day at the office working and take a telephone call from David Barker, Secretary of the Law Society Golf. We chat about the competition and he promises to take care of Tony for me.

Thursday - Tony works until 9.00pm in the evening, preparing dictation tapes and completions for his staff to deal with in his absence.

Friday is another special day, we are attending our friend's son's wedding in Leamington Spa. It is an afternoon wedding and Tony intends to work in the morning. I get a call around midday to say he will be late and for me to go ahead with our friends and he will meet me there. Just before I am due to leave, I get another call to say he probably will not make the wedding service and that he will meet me at the reception. He is having problems with a house completion; a London firm of Solicitors are on the other side and they are being real pains. This is most unusual. Tony never likes to let people down and in particular he always loves the church part of the ceremony, he must be under a lot of pressure at work to cancel the wedding.

I arrive at the church with our friends Lesley, Ray, Gill and Robin. We squeeze into the pew and within minutes people are turning around and mouthing, 'where is Tony?' It is the strangest feeling, I feel a chill run through my body, a premonition. Little do I know this is what the future holds for me, to be on my own.

It is a lovely service and we meet Tony at the Manor Hotel in Meriden. He is apologetic but he is also beaming because he has 'sorted' the arrogant London Solicitors. He can now go away guilt free.

We spend the rest of the afternoon with Tony chatting to many of his nearest and dearest friends. It certainly seems to be a week of celebration and catching up with all our friends. We both love to dance and spend the evening strutting on the dance floor and as the music comes to an end, we have our last dance to Robbie Williams', Angel!

Saturday morning chaos arrives. Oliver has his regular egg date with Daddy. Anthony is busy revising and I am sorting out Tony's packing. Ollie is due to go to a birthday party so I need to get the packing situation under control. As I turn my back, Tony sneaks his favourite pink shirt into my Mum for ironing. He knows it is one I don't like, in fact I thought I had hidden it. But he has found it and Mum laughs as she irons it and adds it to his packing.

Lesley and Ray pull up on the drive to take Tony to the Service Station where he is due to meet Brian Sheridan, his golfing companion, they are travelling together to Stanstead Airport. We hug in the hallway and Tony tells Oliver, 'be good for Mummy'. Oliver laughs and giggles, 'I'm going to sleep in your bed with Mummy whilst you're away'.

He is gone.

Sunday morning and after mass we join Oliver's school friends for a sponsored walk around Berkswell. It is a lovely warm and sunny day, and Mum and I really enjoy the countryside, Oliver enjoys running around with his friends. Poor Anthony is still busy revising for his final exam tomorrow.

We are all tired and Oliver and I spend the evening completing his school project on his favourite holiday destination, Nerja - a part of the Costa del Sol. We have spent many happy holidays in Nerja, the most recent last month. The home telephone rings, 'Hello Sweetheart', Tony has such a lovely voice. He describes his hotel room and the amazing view in great detail, he is overlooking an incredible beach with miles of sand and beautiful blue sea. He tells me how much I would like it, he has just returned from a swim, and how he has had a great practice day on the golf course. He sounds so happy. The competition is due to start tomorrow and he is due to join the guys for dinner soon. He then adds, 'I wish you were here'. I don't think at the time; 'this is odd, he loves being away with his friends, what a strange thing to say' - another premonition.

Tony chats to both boys and then says 'Goodbye, I love you'.

Monday 28th June arrives, just a normal day (my last normal day). I am at the office, Oliver is at school and Anthony is relieved to finish his final exam.

Anthony's friend John arrives and they begin packing. They are excited about their holiday, and Jenny - John's Mum - is due to collect them both the following day to fly off to Spain.

I decide to go to bed early, Oliver is already asleep in my bed. I turn to the boys, 'don't make too much noise you boys, Oliver has school tomorrow'.

With that I go to bed, read for a while and then fall asleep. The next thing I am aware of is my mobile phone ringing...

Chapter 3
So Many Problems

I carry Oliver down the stairs, his arms wrapped tightly around my neck. There is silence in the lounge as everyone waits for us to enter. 'Look who's up', I try to lighten the atmosphere as I drop Oliver onto his feet. He rubs his eyes and seems to squeeze them open and closed as if he is trying to wake up from a bad dream, everyone greets him with uncertain smiles. He looks around the room and makes his way to where Ray is sitting, climbing onto Ray's knee he announces 'Can I watch the cartoons now?' There is a great sigh of relief as Anthony dashes to switch the television on.

I head back upstairs only making it just in time before I am violently sick.

Trying to regain my poise I am aware I need to make another difficult telephone call, this time to Helen. As I hear Helen's voice answer my call I ask her whether Labi is with her, she hesitates for a moment and answers that he is, she knows something is wrong. I am terrified the shock might affect the baby. Typical of Helen, her reaction is instantly one of concern for her brothers, 'Oh my God, how are the boys?' Helen tells me she and Labi will be with us by the end of the day and she offers to be the one to break the news to Victoria and Gerard, my other two step children. Unfortunately, they are both on holiday in different parts of the world. I thank her and know it is time to address the other problems.

The Holiday Insurance - At this stage I am assuming that Tony has died from a heart attack. Tony had suffered a 'mild' heart attack three years ago and he had had a stent fitted. He had not had any other problems since but I am aware that he may not be insured if he has had a heart attack. How will I get him home?

The Office - The staff, Solicitors Regulation Authority (SRA) and the clients will all need to be informed. Who will carry on the Practice?

The Will - The Will should be stored at the office and this will confirm who will head the practice until it is sold. How will I face going back into the office?

Spain - Am I going?

Life seems to be going on around me. People are coming and going, my sister Tina and my nieces, Natasha, Steph, Beth and nephew Tom have arrived and they are playing in the garden with Oliver. I feel like I am in a bubble and my head is hurting, I am trying to think but it hurts, it also still hurts to breathe. People are talking to me and I am aware that I am answering, but I can honestly say, despite having a full house, I have never felt so lonely in all my life!

Brian and Christina Richards arrive, they are very close friends and they are both Solicitors. Brian is already on the phone to the insurers and he is pacing up and down the garden. The doorbell rings again and this time it is my GP, Dr Camm, he had been on Lesley's list of calls to make and bless him he wants to make sure we are all okay. After a quick discussion with Christina, he takes the telephone from Brian and closes the door. I do not know what he is saying to the insurers but he assures me it has been sorted. He hands me a prescription for sleeping tablets or some kind of relaxants, he tells me he doesn't think I will need them, but if I do, to use them. I am desperately trying to keep a clear head, tablets do not seem like a good idea.

As Dr Camm leaves, our accountant Mike Wilson arrives. Mike is also a friend and his grief is apparent. He speaks to Brian and then they both usher me into the lounge. There is a major problem, the office has been contacted but they are unable to locate the Will. They both have their heads in their hands. I have worked in the legal profession since leaving school and I fully understand the significance of finding the Will.

I know what I need to do and agree to be driven to the office to see if I can find the missing Will. I am feeling sick. If I had a choice I would never enter that office again, so many memories. As we walk through the door, Nikki and Yvonne, Tony's Secretaries are both crying, the locum we have employed to cover Tony's holiday, a semi-retired Solicitor is also in tears and obviously out of his depth with the new responsibility. I just feel numb.

The situation is surreal, I find myself in Tony's office looking at his empty chair. Everything is as he left it: His court gown handing on the back of the door; His desk tidy - Tony was always tidy and his files neat and in complete order. It was always a joke with his secretaries that all paper had to be pinned neatly and in line on brass fasteners. Fastidious is the word!

With a heavy heart I begin to search through the filing cabinets for the missing Will. This does not add up, Tony knew the importance of having an up to date Will, we had often discussed it. It is not in the Will file and it is not in our personal files. I begin to panic, where can it be. I decide that just maybe he has left it with our Bank. I walk across the busy road to our bank. Something I do on a daily basis. Today I feel like I am moon walking. I ask to see the Bank Manager and as I explain the situation I see the now familiar shock and sadness on his face. He offers his deepest condolences, but no, they do not have a copy of the Will.

The girls at the office promise to keep searching and we head home empty handed. They are struggling with the dictation tapes. Tony always leaves piles of files and tapes to be worked on. Hearing his voice and knowing he is dead is all too much for them. I shelve the Will problem somewhere in my brain. I have other issues to deal with.

Anthony's friend John has been collected by his Mother and Anthony is emptying his suitcase.

My heart bleeds for him. This is all so unfair. He is very quiet. I am worried about him, how will he cope, how will we all cope?

Young children are so resilient I decide as I watch Oliver still happily playing. You would think it is just any normal day. I don't really know what he is thinking, does he understand what has happened, has it sunk in that he will not see Daddy again?

Opening the door into the kitchen I am overwhelmed by the flowers, cards, messages and food which now covers the surfaces. Mum explains that the doorbell has not stopped and that neighbours, friends and family have been arriving with gifts of every description. So much food! People are just trying to help in whatever way they can. Such kindness.

I am delighted to see the food is being eaten by the boys and other visitors, I am still struggling to swallow. Food is the last thing on my mind and I am grateful that I don't have to think about feeding the boys.

Lesley has notified Oliver's school and the Head Mistress, Mrs Wellings is in shock. An assembly has been called to explain to the children that Oliver's Daddy has died and special prayers are said. As children are being collected from school the word has spread and many of the parents and teachers are in tears.

Many of Oliver's friends are sad and are worried about him, they cling to their parents grateful to have them close. The whole community is affected.

Helen and Labi arrive from London and more decisions need to be made. More telephone calls to and from Spain. I have already been asked whether I am happy for the Golf Competition to continue I did not hesitate - of course it should. Tony would have wanted it to continue.

It is now afternoon and suddenly with all eyes on me I announce that I intend to go to Spain. Anthony enters the room and asks whether he can go with me and I say yes, much to the horror of some of my friends. 'But he is only fifteen, too young to be coping with such a situation'. I disagree, I cannot protect him from this awful situation, it must be his choice. I will decide whether it is appropriate for him to see his Dad's body once we get to Spain. So, it is agreed.

My friend Lesley then volunteers to join us along with Tony's sister, Irene. Victoria is actually in Spain and will meet us at the golfing resort.

I am worried about leaving Oliver, but I know my Mum, sister Tina and all his nieces and nephew have built a cocoon around him. He will be okay.

I suddenly feel very tired and can think no more. A large glass of wine has helped to numb the pain. Ollie and I have waved to the man in the moon, found the brightest star, said our prayers and he is now sleeping. I am not sure what is going through his head, or how much he understands. Today has been a strange day with the house filled with friends and family, all through the day he has constantly watched me to make sure that I am not crying.

Chapter 4
Travelling to Spain

I open my eyes in the early morning sunlight and with a heavy heart I remember yesterday. Oliver's arms are wrapped tightly around my neck. I gently release him and he curls back up into a ball. I kiss his head and leave him sleeping.

Our flight is booked for 2.00pm and we will be away for two nights. I pack a very small bag. It seems really weird, I am usually so fussy about packing, but not today. I actually cannot think about clothes and throw the first things I can put my hands on into the bag. It didn't enter my head that it will be hot in Spain. I pack no sun screen and no make-up. The most important item is my sunglasses not to shield my eyes from the sun, but to shield my eyes from the public. I am not a pretty picture with black circles under my eyes. Robin is driving us to Stanstead Airport where we meet Irene. Irene is Tony's only sister, her eyes are red from crying, we really must look like a strange group amongst all the happy holiday makers. Will I ever feel happy again?

Both Anthony and I manage to laugh as we are ushered through customs, we get through without incident, but both Lesley and Irene have scissors in their bags and are now being searched. Irene makes it worse by announcing she didn't put them there, her husband had packed her bag! They are eventually released and we proceed to the departure lounge. In the past I have always loved shopping in the Duty Free, well you have to buy something. Today I have no interest and sit down feeling like I am in a world all on my own.

Our flight is called and Anthony settles down to read his book. I cannot concentrate and I am fidgeting in my seat. I want to talk to Anthony. He seems content to carry on reading. It's ironic, Anthony is dyslexic and for many years had little interest in books. I had longed for the day when he would read, he is reading now!

I ask him if he is feeling alright and Anthony suddenly turns to me, 'Okay Mummy, I will be fine. I don't like what has happened but we both know we cannot change it. We cannot bring Daddy back. I promise I am not going to turn into a delinquent overnight' and with that he presses the buzzer and calls to the Air Hostess, 'Can you please get my Mum a glass of wine, my Dad has died playing golf in Spain and she is very upset'. The Hostess looks mortified, she returns really quickly with a small bottle of wine and a lemonade for Anthony, she mutters her condolences and said that there will be no charge for the drinks. My son has grown up overnight. I try to settle into the flight but it is no good, my concentration is shot.

I ponder over what the future will hold and that makes my head throb even more.

We land in Cadiz and Brian Sheridan is waiting to meet us. He explains that all the golfers are distraught and offer their condolences. It is the first time something like this has happened and no one really knows what to do. I truly feel saddened for them all, it is a horrible thing to happen, especially on the first day of the competition.

We get into a taxi heading for Novo Sancti Petri in Chiclana de la Frontera. Anthony and I have been before on one of the previous Championships, we had forgotten how remote it is. We are not booked into the same hotel as Brian, where Tony had passed away, we are in one close by. Brian arranges to pick us up the next morning to go to the morgue where he has also arranged a mass in the chapel.

We head to the Restaurant where they are all still trying to make me eat, but I am finding it too difficult. We have a drink on the patio, a piano is playing in the background, and the warm sea-breeze feels comforting. It is too dark to see the view, but I can hear and smell the sea. I close my eyes and pray for normality, I have always loved music, it soothes my head. Unfortunately, the next tune played is Angel and for the first time I feel the tears running down my cheek. I don't try and stop them.

Tiredness begins to take over and we head to our rooms. I am sharing with Anthony, and I am exhausted. Anthony appears from the balcony and says, 'You go to sleep first, I am going to read for a bit on the balcony', I am speechless, he kisses my head and tells me to sleep.

Breakfast is a nightmare, people are happily enjoying their holiday in their swim wear and the sun is shining brighter than ever. I keep my dark glasses on and sip orange juice. Irene and Lesley are forcing different plates of food in front of me in an attempt to make me eat. It isn't going to work - I feel lost.

My stomach is churning with the knowledge that I now have to see Tony. The taxi journey which should be taking fifteen minutes is now over half an hour and Brian is looking edgy. Brian is presented with a hefty taxi bill, he looks at us in disbelief, 'I really don't believe that, we have been ripped off!'. I burst into laughter and the others all think I have gone mad. I explain, whenever we have been on holiday abroad, we always get ripped off by a taxi driver, it was one of the things that always annoyed Tony; It is definitely a sign.

The morgue was not what I was expecting. The building is obviously being renovated, there is scaffolding up, and as we walk inside there are plastic sheets hanging everywhere, with decorators working away painting the walls. A man speaks to Brian and beckons us to follow him, I presume we are going into some sort of chapel of rest. Not so. As we stand in the corridor a door opens and a trolley with Tony's body on it is pushed towards us. There are sudden gasps of horror from Brian, Lesley and Irene as Anthony is dragged back into the direction where we have just come from. I stand staring, at the person in front of me. He is definitely dead. Poor Tony, it is not very dignified, his eyes are wide open as is his mouth and he is wearing nothing but a white sheet. I feel his fingers and touch his cheek, this is not part of the plan, he should be playing golf.

I am horrified that Anthony has been subjected to seeing his Dad like this, but I hadn't been given a choice. Irene returns more composed this time. She gets out some Holy water and begins to bless Tony. I kiss him and say Goodbye.

Back outside in the sunshine Anthony and Lesley still look in shock. They are obviously concerned about me, I manage to smile to reassure them and Anthony looks visibly relieved that I am okay. He tries to tell me that he hadn't seen Tony but we all know that he did, once again he is trying to protect me. I call Victoria and tell her not to come to the morgue. I explained the situation and she instantly agrees that she would rather remember Daddy as he was. We arrange to meet at Tony's Hotel.

We attend the short Mass for Tony. The Priest is a bit stroppy because we are late. We do not share the taxi experience with him.

We are met outside by the Funeral Director, again not quite what I was expecting; very Spanish. He is dressed in tight black trousers, a white shirt unbuttoned showing a very hairy chest and wearing a long gold medallion. He also cannot speak English. Not to be deterred, Lesley calls a friend in Spain and passes the mobile phone to him. It works, we take the mobile back and our friend translates.

There is a lot of confusion as they cannot work out why Tony's name is different to his passport. Oh dear, this will be hard to explain. Tony's birth name was Albert Edward which was what is on his Passport, the name Tony, was his confirmation name and is what he always used as his first name. His travel documents are in the name of Albert, his insurance and hotel booking in the name of Tony. The man looks bemused. Lesley explains to our friend on the phone who translates to the Funeral Director. He suddenly begins to say, 'Si, Si,' but is still looking bemused. He seems satisfied. He also seems very interested in Lesley, he proceeds to kiss her hand several times and she is beginning to look rather uncomfortable when he does not release her hand. Anthony and I began to laugh. Lesley is being hit on by the Funeral Director, only in Spain! I am definitely beginning to feel like we are part of some soap opera and as we make our way to the hotel, I dread to think what Tony's room will be like.

We see Victoria and we embrace - Victoria is 27 and is on holiday with her boyfriend. Despite how she is feeling she puts on a brave face and asks what she can do. I tell her about my fears of entering Tony's room and she says at once that she will go in first. Anthony and the others decide to stay in the reception. I hold my breath as Victoria enters the room. Within seconds she reappears smiling, 'It's fine'. As I enter the room I sense a warm feeling. It does not feel sad. Victoria opens the balcony and the room is filled with sunshine. I sit on the bed. It is just how he described it on the telephone on Sunday night. I smile as I see the pink shirt hanging over the chair. His swimming trunks and towel still drying on the balcony. The sea view is beautiful. Victoria begins the task of packing his clothes while I just sit. It is strange, but I am feeling less dread and breathing seems a bit easier. I suddenly become aware of something rolling from under the bed, it is a golf ball. I pick it up and hold it tightly in my hands - this has to be a sign. The case is almost packed, Victoria smiles at me as she collects his swimming trunks and towel from the balcony, 'messy beggar' and we both laugh. I take his navy-blue Law Society Jacket from the cupboard, he always looked so smart in this. The jacket pocket is heavy, I look inside, £1000 in cash, he never did like credit cards. What a shame he didn't get chance to spend it. I turn and look around the room one more time before closing the door, I wonder briefly how they removed his body. Hotels are busy all night long with people arriving and leaving, did they just wheel him out? Thinking about it, I imagine it probably happens quite a lot, especially with older guests.

As we wheel his suitcase back to our hotel, Anthony stays with Victoria by the pool to talk. Irene goes for a rest. I turn to Lesley, 'I need to walk', we set off along the beautiful beach, miles and miles of golden sand dunes. We feel very conspicuous fully clothed but it does not stop us. We both take off our shoes and we walk through the waves. I am still clutching the golf ball. My trousers are wet, but I don't care. People are staring, everyone else is in swim wear. We walk and then I begin to talk. As if a light bulb has been switched on, I begin to talk, and Lesley just listens. I am going to have the funeral reception at home, it will be a celebration of Tony's life. It will be a garden party, and Oliver will not be afraid, he will be able to play in the garden. I will sell the practice and I will take charge of my life and protect and care for the boys the best way I can. The words just keep coming and we just keep walking.

We walk for two hours and return a bit singed from the sun but I am feeling stronger. As we arrive back at the room Irene meets us, 'Something terrible has happened'. I look at her and think - as long as my boys are safe what can be more terrible - 'the office has called, the SRA has frozen all of your office/client bank accounts'. I shrug my shoulders, 'it's fine, I will deal with them when I get home'.

Chapter 5
Taking Control

As we wait for the baggage to come out at Stanstead Airport, I feel a sudden sadness as I watch Anthony lift his Dad's suitcase from the conveyor belt. I had already had a bit of a moment on the plane when I thought I caught a glimpse of the back of Tony's head. It wasn't Tony of course, but for that short time I had forgotten he was dead.

Robin greets us with the car and we head home. My mobile rings and it is Mum. She wants to pre-warn me that the Coventry Evening Telegraph has covered the story of Tony's death and it is in today's paper. I wince and ask her to read it to me. She tells me that there is a nice photograph of Tony. I knew it would be public news, Tony was well liked and respected as a Solicitor, School Governor and Trustee of the St. Bernadette Trust. Seeing it in print suddenly makes it real.

We arrive home and Oliver runs to open the door, 'Mummy, Mummy, come and see all my letters, can I go to Edwards house? Can I go to the Summer Fayre? He hands me a letter and I summon up all my strength not to cry.

Dear Oliver,

I'm sorry to hear about your Daddy, I hope you can come and play soon. Mummy said you can come for a sleepover. Please ring me if you feel lonely.

Love Edward

I cannot read anymore. 'Of course, I will telephone Edward's Mummy.'

I had also completely forgotten about the School Summer Fayre this coming Sunday. I am joint Chairperson with my dear friend Anne O'Brien. The Summer Fayre is the hardest event to run all year and I have abandoned poor Anne. I make a quick call to Anne who confirms she has everything under control and that the committee have been really supportive. She is more concerned about me and arranges to come to see me later in the day.

Mum and my sister Tina have done a great job of looking after Oliver and he seems fine, if not a little over excited. I tell them of our experiences in Spain and they look horrified. Oliver comes to sit on my knee, 'Did you see Daddy?', I try and explain the best way I can, that we had seen Daddy's body but that he was already in heaven. I tell him all about the lovely beach, sea and swimming pool, Oliver loves to swim. I wanted him to know that the place where his Daddy died is not horrible and frightening but beautiful, 'I will take you and show you one day' I promise.

I turn my attention to the office and explain to Mum that I need some time to sort things out. Bless her, she does not realise how serious the situation is as she tells me that I need to rest.

I lock myself into our home office, take a deep breath and begin. I call our Accountant and Brian and Christina to ascertain my legal rights. I make the dreaded call to the SRA and confirm a meeting with them at the office on Monday morning. I call the Bank Manager and he agrees to put mirror accounts in place so that the practice can continue to run. This is a very costly exercise, but the only way we can continue to run the practice. I call the girls at the office and arrange for them to come to the house on Sunday for a meeting. I read down my list of messages and call in favours from people who have offered their help including Michael Hammon - the Senior Partner of a firm of Solicitors near to the office, he agrees to do whatever he can to help. I call my Accountant back and he agrees to attend a meeting at the house on Sunday. Lastly, I call Helen and Labi to ask if they can be part of the meeting.

I don't recognise the person who has just taken control, I have never dealt with Lawyers, Bank Managers, Accountants and especially the SRA, that was Tony's job. I have found a new hidden strength and I congratulate myself on sounding so confident. I close the office door to spend time with my family and try and close off my mind to the mounting problems.

I wake up early on Saturday morning and Mum is not happy when I say I am going to the office. She is worried and tells me I shouldn't go on my own. The office is closed and I need the time to make sure the accounts are up to date for the meeting on Monday. I switch off my emotions as I enter the office and make my way to the accounts office upstairs. I spend the morning working and feel confident that everything is in order. As I close the office door several of the neighbours greet me, they must have seen my car parked outside. Tony was well liked in the area and I am given flowers and cards. I thank everyone for their kindness and head home.

Sunday arrives and we go to Mass in Kenilworth. We have a lovely parish in Balsall Common but I just cannot face so many people asking me if we are okay, I want to be invisible. Christina has agreed to take Oliver to the school Summer Fayre and he is excited about seeing all his friends. I am grateful to have the house to myself as I prepare for the important meeting about to take place.

Yvonne and Nikki arrive from the office they are relieved that Oliver is out, they confess to not knowing what to say to him. I smile and tell them he is coping well as long as people do not cry. They both burst into tears!

The others arrive and Mum makes tea. I confirm that the Will still hasn't been found and so this means Tony has died intestate. Everyone in the room is shocked because Tony was such a great Solicitor and all his other paperwork was in complete order. This leaves us as a family having to deal with a very complicated and stressful situation at a time when all we want to do is come to terms with his death.

It is decided that Helen and I will become Administrators of the Estate. Thankfully, it is ascertained that the house is in joint names and automatically passes to me as is Tony's SIPP Fund. The rest of the Estate which includes the sale of the business and the office premises will need to go to Probate.

The next problem is the pending SRA visit tomorrow morning. Brian explains the seriousness of the situation to everyone in the room. The fact they have the right to 'intervene'.

An Intervention by the Solicitors Regulation Authority

An intervention takes place when the SRA closes down a solicitor's practice. This power is given by Parliament and it enables them to take from the firm documents and money that belongs to clients. They only intervene in the Public Interest.

An intervened firm is completely closed down. It is no longer able to act for its clients. Usually, a specialist firm of solicitors is hired to help close down a practice and such firms are called SRA intervention agents.

The room is silent, this would mean that the staff lose their jobs immediately and the Estate would be charged an astronomical amount of money for the privilege. I could possibly even lose the house to pay the costs.

It is madness, everyone knew that it was Tony's wishes that Brian Richards would take over the practice, where in God's name is the Will? How dare Tony die and leave us in this mess? The feeling of anger is a new emotion. I have felt numb, sad, tearful, breathless and now angry.

I tell the girls that I will do everything in my power to protect their jobs and to retain the Practice until it can be sold. Brian agrees to be present at the meeting arranged for tomorrow together with Michael Hammond and I am just going to pray in the meantime.

Lesley and Ray have invited us to Sunday dinner which is a blessing as food is still the last thing on my mind. The children would have starved if it had not been for family and friends. We head to their house together with Brian, and Christina and Oliver arrive back from their afternoon of fun. Christina tells me everyone has been so kind and Oliver had been happy spending time with his friends. I decide it is time for Oliver to return to school tomorrow, he needs his friends. Anthony has been with friends and also arrives. It feels like a celebration but we all know it isn't.

As we finish eating Brian excuses himself from the table to take a telephone call. He returns to the room and whispers in my ear, 'he's home'. Pargetters Funeral Directors had met the flight at Birmingham airport and had taken charge of Tony's body. I can feel the tears welling up and my stomach turning as Anthony squeeze's my hand. But as Oliver's worried face turns to me, I bite my lip so hard in an effort not to cry I can taste blood.

The most important thing is, he's home.

Chapter 6
The SRA

Considering my life has been turned upside down I am amazed that I am sleeping so well. My brain is that exhausted by the end of the day that I just close my eyes and I sleep.

Morning has come too soon and at 6.00am I get myself into power mode by dressing in my most formal suit. It is a bit hot and it is obvious that I have lost quite a bit of weight in the last week as the suit is hanging off me. Never mind, it will do.

Mum promises to get Oliver ready for school and I leave with my briefcase. Is this really me or has an imposter taken over my life?

I arrive at the office for 8.00am and calmly make coffee, just like any normal day. Today is not a normal day though, today I find out what our future holds. My stomach turns and I tip the coffee away opting for water. Yvonne and Nikki arrive early followed by Brian and Michael.

At 9.00am on the dot. The SRA representative arrives. He's only a young man and I find myself feeling quite sorry for him. He actually looks more uncomfortable than I do. I introduce him to the girls and explain their roles within the firm. I then introduce Brian and Michael and explain that they are present in a supportive role and then I explain my role in the business and I ask him if he would like to see the accounts first. I explain that we not only have a computer accounting system but that Tony also liked to keep his own manual system up to date as he did not trust computers. I confirmed both were up to date. I thought he might find this a bit silly but he actually said he thought it was a good idea as computers do have a tendency to go wrong. He thanked me and said it was not necessary to look at them.

He then begins the meeting by asking me if I understand why he is here and whether I understand what an intervention is and that he does have the authority to intervene.

I can feel my stomach churning again and pray that I will not be sick.

I take a deep breath and suddenly find the speech I have made in my head being manifested into words. 'Yes, I do understand both questions, but do you understand that my husband has not yet been buried, my sons aged 7 and 15 are being cared for by my Mother and I am in this office protecting the clients welfare'? I go on to say that although I am not a Solicitor, I understand the accounting rules and that I have the most incredible support staff any firm could have. I also have the professional support of two well respected local Solicitors who have promised to continue this support as long as it is required. Brian and

Michael both nod their heads in agreement. They do not speak and I am hoping it is because I have said the right things.

I finish off by telling him that if it is so important for a Sole Practitioner to require a Will, then the SRA clearly should hold a copy on file! That said I shut up.

I realise that it does matter to me that our clients are taken care of properly. People who have instructed a Solicitor are usually going through a stressful situation such as divorce, moving house or probate and they are putting all their trust into their chosen firm of Solicitors to get the job done.

The room has gone quiet and then as I look directly at the man from the SRA I realise he has tears in his eyes. Not what I was expecting. It is a jolly good job Oliver is not here.

I realise I am holding my breath as he begins to speak. The relief washes over me when he confirms that he does not feel an intervention is necessary in this case and that as long as I can commit my time to the firm until it is sold then the practice can remain open until a buyer is found. He stipulates that we will need to get a full-time locum solicitor on the premises and that both Brian and Michael will need to act as supervisors.

With that he stands up and shakes my hand, he offers his sincere condolences and leaves.

We celebrate our reprieve and begin the job of looking for Locums and Buyers for the practice. We try Warwickshire Law Society, no luck they do not have any names of locums on record and cannot help. We then go onto Birmingham Law

Society who only have one person available but the problem is that he only specialises in Employment Law. Oh dear! We decide to take the one man who is available with the view that his job is just to be present at the office for compliance purposes. Solicitor friends agree to cover, and the girls are more than capable with dealing with most client matters. I have the accounts covered and know my responsibility to the clients.

A letter is drafted and sent out to all Coventry Solicitors telling them that we are urgently looking for a buyer.

Life does go on.

Chapter 7
The Funeral

With Tony's body now home, I can concentrate on the funeral. So many unanswered questions still. I have a Death Certificate but I need to find an interpreter because it is in Spanish.

Things are still not going to plan. Tony had always told me that he wanted to be buried at Temple Balsall Cemetery where his still born son Paul Anthony is buried. In fact, he had purchased a plot of land. I hand the piece of paper to the funeral directors and I receive a call to say that the burial plot is only big enough for a baby grave and there are no spaces at the cemetery for him to be buried. Oh!

I next contact Berkswell Churchyard, this is next to Oliver's lovely village school, Berkswell Church of England School. Thankfully we live on the right side of Meeting House Lane to be classed as Berkswell residents, result.

Arrangements are made for the funeral to be on held on Tuesday 13th July at St Francis Of Assisi Church in Kenilworth followed by burial at Berkswell Churchyard. I arrive home and look at the calendar on the wall, oh no, yet another problem; this date is Sports Day at Berkswell School and it will be directly next to the Churchyard. It will be too distressing for the children, and the village will be full of cars - we will be unable to get the funeral cars through.

I make the telephone call to Mrs Wellings at Berkswell School. I apologise profusely and she tells me to stop. She assures me that the situation will be sorted and I am to stop worrying. Sure, to her word, Oliver arrives home with a note in his bag informing all parents that Sports Day has been postponed due to unforeseen circumstances. I am feeling very guilty!

I next receive a call from the interpreter; Tony had not died of a heart attack, he had died from an Abdominal Aortic Aneurysm. A condition which is common in men and cannot be diagnosed unless a scan has taken place. It also cannot be repaired without open-heart surgery.

Abdominal Aortic Aneurysm - symptoms that your aortic aneurysm has ruptured may include sudden, intense back pain, which can be described as a tearing sensation.

The Doctor confirms to me that Tony would have been dead before he hit the floor, the moment the Abdominal Aortic Aneurysm ruptured he would have died instantly. I feel some comfort that he did not suffer.

As a family we make the arrangements for the funeral service, we all know this would have been really important to Tony as his faith meant everything to him. It feels good to have all the children at home. Labi, Gerard and Anthony declare they are going to be pallbearers, I am extremely proud but also saddened that Anthony at fifteen is going to carry his Dad's coffin. Helen and Anthony are to do the readings, and Gerard and Victoria are to do the bidding prayers. Oliver immediately says that he wants a job so it is agreed that Oliver and I will take the offertory and between us we choose the hymns. Irene and John take charge of the funeral order of service and I have already asked Brian Richards and Tony Cotterill to do the Eulogy.

I turn my attention to the wake. With the help of Anne O'Brien, caterers and portaloos are booked, flower arrangements for tables are being arranged and a bar for the garden. This will be a send-off to remember, it will also feel like a garden party and Oliver can run around and hopefully not be too sad or frightened.

The week has been bizarre, I have worked every day at the office as promised and I feel guilty. I feel as if the boys have lost a Mummy as well as a Daddy as I am out of the house at eight and back at six. Thank heavens for my Mum. The office is to close on the day of the funeral as a mark of respect and also so that the staff can all attend.

Monday evening arrives and Tony's body is to be received into church at 7.00pm. I have arranged for the coffin to be brought into the house before we leave for church. I need him to come home.

It is also really important to me that Oliver gets to see the coffin close up and in private. The only memories I have of my Dad's funeral, when I was the same age as Oliver, is seeing the coffin for the first time in church. It terrified me. I can remember my Mum clutching my hand so tightly it hurt.

We are all waiting in the hallway as the hearse draws to a holt outside the house and the coffin is carefully wheeled into the hallway. It feels surreal. It's a big, heavy cast-iron coffin. Earlier in the week I had got myself all upset because I wanted to choose a different coffin. Ridiculous really, considering everything that is happening, I have a blip over the coffin. The funeral directors calmly and kindly explained that Tony could not be moved from the coffin he was in because of the conditions his body had been kept in. I understood.

We begin to say a prayer and then I encourage Oliver to touch the coffin. He is not scared, he touches the coffin and he seems comfortable in its presence. I kiss the coffin and we all say our own personal farewell before I signal the funeral directors we are ready to go.

There are two cars following the hearse and, as we pull out of the drive, I am overwhelmed to see many of the neighbours standing at the side of the road. He was certainly well loved.

Oliver seems excited by the travel arrangements. He suddenly pipes up with, 'Is there a mini bar in this limousine?' I apologise to the driver who is trying his hardest not to laugh. Not to be silenced Oliver then says, 'Excuse me driver, can this car please go faster, my Daddy didn't like slow drivers'! We all laugh, I am glad it feels relaxed.

I am amazed at the amount of people attending the reception service and I am glad that Oliver seems to be coping well. In the church lots of people line up to offer their condolences and prayers as they shake hands or hug each member of the family. We leave to go home and Oliver insists in getting in the first car with Labi. We are all in the second car and head home. As we pull up onto the drive I am aware that the first car is now behind us. As I get to the door I am floored when I hear Oliver shout at the top of his voice, 'you f****** beat us'. We all gasp and Labi looks like he is about to pass out as does the driver of the car. 'Oliver McAtamney get into the house NOW', I order, my voice shaking. The others are laughing and trying for Oliver not to see them, I look very stern. Oliver doesn't seem to know what he has done wrong. As I take him into the house and sit him on my knee I ask where he has heard such language. He admits he has been watching Anthony's Futurama DVD's without anyone knowing. I feel guilty yet again. I should be at home with him, not working. I give him a hug and explain that it is a bad word and not to say it again. He promises he will not and I confiscate the offending DVD's. A large glass of wine is most definitely in order.

The morning of the funeral arrives, the sun is shining and the house and garden is a flurry of activity, my friends and family are incredible. Gazebos, tables and chairs are arriving and the garden is looking at its best. The posh portaloos are parked on the drive and the caterers are busy. We could be preparing for a birthday, wedding or christening but today, it is a celebration of life.

I really feel like I am disconnected from the real world, that I am outside looking in on someone else's life. I feel a great sadness, but this is numbed by my passion to make sure that today goes well. We are making a memory which will be with us all of our lives and it has to be special. I want Tony to be remembered for the wonderful, loving person he was. He touched so many people's lives and this is becoming more apparent as each day goes by, the many letters and cards received I know will comfort me in the months and years to come.

I am dressed in black and have decided on the accessory of a black wide brimmed hat, it makes me feel that I can hide from the world. I am just taking a few moments to compose myself before joining the children downstairs.

As the funeral cars pull up on the drive, I take a deep breath, it's time to go.

The family is split into two cars and we are quietly reflecting on the service ahead. As we pull into the church car park it is obvious that there are already hundreds of people in attendance. Oliver seems slightly overwhelmed by the crowds of people and he squeezes my hand. I smile down at him for reassurance and we walk to our seats next to Tony's coffin. For a moment I feel like I am going to pass out. I am sure everyone must be able to smell the coffin, there seems to be some sickly odour in the air. Nobody else seems to be noticing, perhaps I am imagining it.

The smell gets deflected as the service begins and the many, many priests begin to fill the alter. I have never seen so many priests at one time. Tony had attended Cotton College, a Roman Catholic Boarding School in Staffordshire and many of his friends had joined the Priesthood. Each priest is swinging a thurible filled with incense from side to side, the alter is filled with smoke. After a few seconds our ears are filled with the penetrating shrill of the fire alarm. Oh dear!

Everyone is told to remain calm whilst the alarm is switched off, I cannot believe something else has gone wrong and Helen whispers to me, 'if he is not careful, he is going to be cremated'. We laugh, because we all knew Tony wishes were to be buried, but everything just seemed to be going wrong.

The service resumes with some beautiful hymns and Helen is the first to read. Labi stands by her side for support. A reading from the prophet Isaiah - The Lord will destroy death forever. Helen speaks with confidence and reverence.

It is soon Anthony's turn to read. I feel sick for him; will he be okay? A reading from the letter of St Paul to the Romans - Alive or dead, we belong to the Lord. He reads beautifully.

We all sit and listen to the Homily given by Father Kevin - it is very moving.

Victoria and Gerard continue with the bidding prayers and one of Tony's favourite hymns is sung, Here I am Lord. Oliver and I collect the offertory,

Oliver carefully carrying the bread as I carry the wine. He looks very important.

As I look around I am amazed at the people in attendance, there is a swarm of yellow sweatshirts on one side of the church - the St. Bernadette Trust, Tony had been a Trustee for many years and it is lovely to see so many of the sick and handicapped children. I also recognise many clients, solicitors, neighbours, teachers and golfers together with friends and family. He was certainly well loved.

After communion Tony Cotterill and Brian Richards begin the Eulogy, two of his oldest and dearest friends. They begin to speak and soon we are all laughing and smiling at some of the antics being told. They are doing a fantastic job. I know it has been particularly difficult for them because in talking about Tony's life it is also important that Tony's ex-wife Sheelagh is mentioned, the Mother of Helen, Victoria and Gerard. She is at the service along with her parents and I did not want them to feel left out or awkward in any way. I need not have worried, they did him proud.

As the final prayer and hymn starts, I feel immense grief as the boys move towards lifting the coffin onto their shoulders. Anthony and Gerard are at the front and I can tell how heavy the coffin is. I am so proud of them both. Oliver is staring at me as we move behind the coffin, I must not cry. He holds my hand as we walk slowly, all eyes are on us and many people are crying - I will stay strong.

For a moment the image of Princes William and Harry comes into my head, them walking behind their Mother's coffin, how brave they were. No child should have to do this.

I am relieved to be back in the car and heading for Berkswell Churchyard, Tony's final resting place. I know we are causing a massive traffic jam with people trying to follow the funeral procession. The driver asks us to wait in the car whilst people catch up.

This has to be the hardest bit, the internment. I hold Oliver close to me as the coffin is lowered into the ground and I am fighting back the tears. In the distance I can hear the children from Oliver's school playing in the playground and in some ways, this gives me reassurance and comfort. I hand Anthony and Oliver red roses and they each drop them on top of the coffin. Mum leads Oliver away as I say my final farewell.

I am handed a glass of wine as we arrive home. It is lovely to see so many people. The celebration of life goes on late into the night. He would have loved it!

Chapter 8

Life goes on

As family and friends return to their lives, I feel a sense of despair and panic. I have focused on the funeral since Tony's death and now I am feeling lost.

Work has become my salvation in the week, it is the weekends I struggle with. I can lose myself at work, I can become someone else. I know Mum is finding this difficult as well, she thinks I should be home more. She is of course right, but I don't really have an option at the moment. If I am honest, I am happier away from home. Home doesn't feel the same any more. At home the realisation that Tony is never coming back is hard. I always loved the weekends but now they feel full of loneliness. I still listen for the key to turn in the lock and the familiar voice calling out, "I'm home darling, have you had a good day?". They were not just words, he really did want to hear about my day, even if we had worked together.

It is now the school holidays and I am very lucky that Oliver has so many friends. He has been invited out most days. Most nights he clings to me before going to sleep but he still likes to go for sleep overs with friends. These are the nights I cry myself to sleep.

The weekends are hard for him, I can tell this is when he misses Daddy. He was sad at the end of term because all the Daddy's were in attendance for the assembly at school, I feel helpless.

Anthony is busy preparing for his new school. He is due to start the Sixth Form at the Heart of England School. This is a blessing in disguise, Anthony had made this decision before Tony's death, he wanted to be able to get to and from school under his own steam and not be dependent on lifts or buses. We still have to collect his GCSE results from Princethorpe College at the end of August.

We also have a celebration - he will be sixteen on the 30th of July. Thankfully, there have only been a few people making silly remarks like, "You're the man of the house now "and "you need to take care of your mother and brother".

Work is frantic, with no sign of a buyer despite lots of promises. It is costing me a fortune to run the mirrored accounts and pay for locums. I have no personal finance as the accounts are still frozen whilst going through probate. I am lucky to have good friends who are supporting me financially!

I have to say I am quite surprised, I have not heard from the Solicitors Benevolent Association. Tony had supported this charity since he qualified as a Solicitor - indeed, we had always attended many social events over the years. Not quite sure where they are now when they are needed?

SBA The Solicitors 'Charity is an independent charity working for solicitors both past and present and their families. Every year we help hundreds of people of all ages who are in serious financial need as a result of illness, accident, redundancy or other adversity.

Oh well, perhaps our need is not considered great enough although it would be nice to be asked if we need help!

At least when I am at work, people have stopped asking if I am okay. It is strange, when I am at home, I have stopped going to the village shops as I am finding people crossing the road as if they are embarrassed to speak to me or I see people pointing and whispering. To be honest I have stopped going out locally full stop.

Today is Anthony's Birthday and he is now sixteen. The family and friends are rallying again, and a barbeque has been arranged. The garden is full of laughter as Anthony's friends surround him with best wishes. The loss feels greater than ever as we all try to fill the missing gap. It is only just over a month but to be fair it feels like forever.

Good news beckons as we manage to secure a sale. It won't be quick, but at least we can get rid of the locums. Our accounts will remain mirrored until the final contract is signed and that could be some time, but at least the responsibility has been lifted from me. I must remain with the practice until the sale is completed, but at least the office can run under their Practicing Certificate and legal staff.

The day has arrived to collect Anthony's exam results, my friend Marlene collects us both and we drive over to Princethorpe. I feel the familiar stomach churning. Not only do we have to face staff and parents most of whom I haven't seen since the funeral, but I also worry for Anthony. He is dyslexic, and I really don't know how he will have done. To think, before Tony's death my big worry in life was that Anthony was dyslexic and Oliver possibly too. Now this seems insignificant, as long as the boys are emotionally stable, I am happy. I do wish Tony was with me though to hold my hand.

Marlene and I stand back as we watch the boys open the brown envelope handed to them. I can hardly bare to look. I then see the smile spread across Anthony's face, he has passed all his exams with flying colours and can take up his place in the new Sixth Form - I cry.

Now we have been taken over I can at least take some time out. We are booked to share a gite in France with Lesley and Ray and their grand-daughters. The booking was made before Tony's death. I have invited Anthony's friend John to join us as we now have a spare place, plus the boys had already missed out on their trip to Spain.

I still have no money but again this doesn't matter because my friends have taken care of it. I now have a long list of money I owe people, how embarrassing. I hope the probate is sorted soon.

Oliver decides to travel with Lesley and Ray and the girls, so I have just the older boys in my car. All seems well until we hit the port and I realise that I have to drive the big Mercedes onto the ferry. I am terrified. Anthony tells me that we will probably be on the bottom layer and not to worry. No such luck. I am directed to the upper level of the ferry having to negotiate bends and bumps. In the end I just go for it and feel extremely proud to park up in my allocated space without taking the side of the car out.

Our first holiday without Tony. It is difficult for us all because we miss him terribly. I do relax and thanks to my lovely friends we all manage to enjoy the holiday. I could not have done it without their support blanket cushioning the pain.

We arrive home refreshed after 10 days. Although Anthony and John accuse me of child abuse as the only music, I have in the car is Tom Jones! Good old Tom.

School life begins again, and the dark nights start to set in. I hate it. I feel trapped and Christmas is coming. Christmas has always been my favourite time of year. Now I am dreading it.

Thankfully, after a lot of stamping of feet and yelling down the telephone by my friend Marlene, who is an accountant, Tony's SIPP fund is released to me. What a relief. The bank accounts at the office are still mirrored and the Probate has gone quiet. But I can pay my debts and breathe again financially.

Things are not going great at the office. Although I am grateful for the new firm coming in, it is hard - they are not treating our clients the same way as Tony did. We are receiving lots of complaints and the staff are leaving one by one.

They just cannot stand by and watch the firm changing in this way.

We hold a lot of Lasting Power of Attorney's and Tony was a wonderful attorney. He didn't charge unless he physically had to do something and always visited his clients with flowers on their birthday; the new firm are billing monthly. It is becoming harder to stay quiet, but I know it is necessary, and no longer my business to interfere. However, my temper explodes when I arrive at the office to find Tony's court gown flung on the floor with a pile of rubbish. A young, arrogant training Solicitor is clearing the office and has no idea that I might be hurt or offended by his actions. He got the message, I immediately took the precious garment home, I did not wash it. I ironed it and hung it in my wardrobe - my special keepsake.

Oliver seems to be coping, but I am aware that he is putting on weight - comfort eating. Mum is trying to keep an eye on his eating, but it is difficult.

I am seeing a change in Anthony as well. He loves his new school and seems to be making new friends. He has a school trip to visit the Houses of Parliament and I advise him to wear a suit. When he arrives, everyone else is dressed in jeans, but it certainly catches the attention of the young ladies. Suddenly he has a glint in his eye, and every other word is Kara!

As Christmas comes closer, I really wish I could fast forward and miss it completely, but that would not be fair on the boys.

We have Christmas lunch with friends, yet again Lesley and Ray have rescued us. Mum is wonderful holding everything together at home. We have my sister's family on Boxing Day.

I have made the decision to go away with our friends to France for New Year. This was another trip already in the diary before Tony died. Anthony has chosen to stay at home with Nanny (and Kara). Ollie and I pack our bags and join our friends on the Euro Tunnel to France. Another first for me - I have been through the Tunnel with Tony, but this time I am driving. Our friend Gill insists on being a passenger just in case I get lost in France. She is a French teacher so that would obviously help as I do not speak very much French.

We meet up with the others at the Gite. New Year is always emotional, but this year is particularly poignant. I feel like I am galloping through life at the moment, I suppose just trying to survive. I really don't know who I am anymore.

At the start of the New Year, I finally manage to get the sale Contract signed and I can hand over the Client Accounts. The office Account is released and I can pass it over to our probate lawyers.

Although I am still contracted to the office for the time being, I begin to plan my next move; I decide to set up my own Recruitment Agency. I plan a meeting with Warwickshire Law Society and agree to work in association with them to provide Locums and Permanent legal staff. This was the one thing which was not available in my time of need and I certainly could see the gap in the market.

In May I decide to leave the practice completely. I soon have my own offices and by June, Warwickshire Legal Recruitment Ltd is opened to the public. I love running the agency, it is so rewarding to make a successful placement or just be able to provide holiday or sick cover for firms struggling with staff problems.

Whilst this side of my life seems to be going well, I also discover in August that the firm which has taken over the legal practice has not paid any rent into our probate account or any commission for the entire time it has been in situ. They have the option to buy the offices as part of the contract, but nothing has happened. They have me tied in knots! I trusted these people, I thought they were my friends!

I have taken my eye off the ball and now the estate is in trouble. My Solicitor should have pointed this out, but he has his own problems to deal with by way of a hostile takeover of his firm. I realise I need help. I realise I am losing control and I hate it.

It is strange how things work out. During this period, I have been doing what I do best, fundraising! Tony was a former Governor at the primary school next to the office, Sacred Heart Roman Catholic School. I heard they were trying to raise funds for a sensory garden area for the children to play. They require £10,000.00. I have automatically offered to organise a Charity Ball at the Ricoh Arena in Coventry. The Ricoh is a new venue and the first concert is on 23rd September 2015 with the amazing Bryan Adams - our Ball is booked a week later. The support has been amazing with many Solicitors donating in memory of Tony. It will be an amazing event.

I am contacted by Steve, a Solicitor from a Birmingham based firm. Steve was a friend of Tony's, and he apologises for not being able to attend the forthcoming Ball but offers a donation. He asks if I am okay and for the first time, I admit I need help. I ask if he knows a good Litigation Lawyer preferably in Birmingham as I did not want a Coventry firm. Bless him - he replies, "will I do"? I spill out all my problems and within an hour or so, he has taken control and a plan of action is in place.

I am frustrated and angry. The loss of control has not been good for my health and once again my weight starts to plummet. I really do need to regain control. The plans for the Ball are going well and we have 260 tickets sold for the event, but I am nervous because I also know the partners from the takeover firm will be present. I need to be civilised. I need to carry the event off without any issues.

I need not have worried, as the evening runs to plan and is a huge success. I even manage to thank everyone including the firm I am at logger-heads with. We raise just under £7000.00 enough for the school to begin the work on the sensory garden immediately.

I am happy, Tony would have been very proud of the achievement and it is a lovely way for the school and local community to remember him.

Sunday is a day of rest, but I am agitated as I know I have a job to do tomorrow to regain my control and protect the Estate. I am nervous but equally excited that at last something positive is about to happen.

Steve picks me up at 2.00pm from my Recruitment offices and asks if I am ready - I am. We drive first to my former office where I walk in and ring the bell. I ask for the partner and as he approaches the desk, I serve him notice from my new firm of Solicitors. It is brilliant - his face drops and I walk out. On to the next office and again I serve notice on the second partner. Steve looks at me as I get back into the car. I feel two foot taller and my adrenalin is running fast! He smiles and shakes his head, "I think we have created a monster".

It certainly had worked. By the time we get home, Steve's office has called to say the fax machine has been whizzing out letters in their defence. The silence and their control is broken, and they are now panicked.

Needless to say, by the end of November all the rent, commission, and finally the purchase is complete and all monies in our probate account. I felt free, I will always be indebted to Steve.

Although my experience with the practice who took over my firm had its problems, I am very grateful and mindful that they did take it over, so many firms promised and did not come forward. At the end of the day the business problems were sorted, and I am happy to say we have remained friends.

Chapter 9
Moving On

It has taken approximately eighteen months but finally the estate is completed, and life begins to feel more settled.

I am enjoying Warwickshire Legal Recruitment and it has given me the flexibility to be home more for Oliver. I can take him to school and on many days, I will collect him also.

I recently received a call from school, from a visiting special needs teacher, she wanted to tell me that Oliver is dyslexic, and did I realise. I explain that I am not surprised but that his emotional welfare is more important to me at the moment. She is concerned because she sees how bright and intelligent Oliver is, and that he does not seem to be getting the right assistance at school. I thank her and assure her that I will know when the time is right to push matters at school. For now, it is enough that he is happy.

I am concerned though, he is putting on weight and although he is now back sleeping in his own bed, I have to leave a light on in his room. He also questions where I am and how long I will be when

I go out anywhere. He doesn't like plans to change in any way.

I know he misses male company in particular. Lots of relatives made promises following Tony's death to take him out and show him some attention, but as the time goes by everyone is busy getting on with their own lives.

I decide to ask one of his uncle's if he is free to take Oliver to a football match or swimming, or bowling. It is the only time I have asked, and I am taken aback when he says that he is too busy. I make the decision not to ask again.

It is strange that people make promises to children and then do not keep them! One relative promised to arrange driving lessons for Anthony, again this has not happened. Other friends have invited the boys and I for Sunday lunch - it doesn't matter to me that it never happens, but Oliver keeps asking when we are going? Small things can mean a lot to young children.

I decide that perhaps it is time to get Oliver some counselling.

We are very lucky, Dr Camm puts us in contact with a Counselling Service called the Lighthouse. They do not usually deal with children but have agreed to make some enquiries to find a suitable Counsellor. A Counsellor is found, and she has agreed to do some sessions with Oliver. The Lighthouse is a charity, so although the sessions are free, they do rely on donations to continue. I am more than happy to donate.

The Counsellor asks Oliver whether he is happy to stay on his own with her and he agrees. I tell him I will be back in half an hour. He seems quite comfortable with me leaving and I am relieved. I disappear for a coffee. I am called back into the room and Oliver shows me a drawing he has done. The Counsellor explains to me that the drawing is of his family and the people he feels closest to.

At the top is Labi, Gerard and Anthony, they are stood with Oliver. Further down is Mummy, Nanny, Helen and Victoria. Next to them is his Aunty Tina, my sister with his cousins Natasha, Stephanie, Beth and Tom. The Counsellor asks who everyone is. It becomes quite obvious that the males in the family are really important to him. Nanny and I are the centre of his world and his sisters are next to us, my sister's family are really important too. She asks Oliver if Tina has a husband because there is not one on the drawing, he says yes and leaves it at that. He obviously does not see him as important in his life and so does not deserve a place on his drawing!

The Counsellor starts to build a memory box with Oliver. Each week we go they will add something to it.

On the second session Oliver reveals that he does not trust anything his brother tells him. He tells the Counsellor that Anthony did not tell him the truth the night his Daddy died. I am shocked. The Counsellor explains that Anthony had told Oliver that everything was alright, and that Mummy just had toothache. In Oliver's world now, if Anthony tells him that Mummy has just gone to the shops or that she is out with friends, he does not believe him. He fears I might be dead or not coming back. I am really shocked. It had seemed like the right and easiest thing to do, not tell Oliver until the morning, but obviously this has been troubling him.

This is a real lesson to me - no matter how difficult it seemed we should have told him the truth immediately. I feel I have let him down. The Counsellor explains to Oliver that adults do not always get it right and on that occasion, we were all trying to protect him. I make a promise to Oliver that we will always tell him the truth in future.

On the third session the Counsellor tackles the question of Mummy not being allowed to cry. She explains to Oliver that everyone needs to cry sometimes. He disagrees and says that he does not want Mummy to cry, it makes him sad. He does not want Mummy to be sad. She quietly explains to Oliver that he must give Mummy permission to cry. Oliver still doesn't seem convinced.

After the final session the Counsellor tells me that she feels Oliver is coping well. He has completed his Memory Box and can take it home. She looks at me and says, I don't feel that Oliver requires any further counselling but that she is pretty sure that I do! 'In time', I tell her, 'when the time feels right'.

Anthony appears to be thriving, but he never really talks about his Dad's death and this does worry me. I am absolutely delighted when he is made Head Boy in his second year in the Sixth Form, and I know his Dad would have been proud. I am sad he is not here to see it.

Anthony does share one blip with me. He tells me he has walked out of a drama lesson at school. Apparently, the teacher had told the class to put themselves in a dark place, the worst place they could think of, or to relive the worst experience of their lives. Anthony told me, he couldn't open that box and that he just left the classroom. The teacher wasn't to know his history.

I am invited to become a Parent Governor at Oliver's School and I decide that this is a really good way to keep an eye on him from a distance, and give something back to the school for all the care and kindness shown to Oliver in the period since Tony's death.

At last I am beginning to feel happy at home. Of course, there is still a massive hole in my life, but home is beginning to feel like home again.

Lots of people keep asking why I stay in the same house. For one thing, Mum is in the Granny Flat, it would be wrong to move her again and why cause the boys any further trauma by more change? They love their home, they have their memories and they feel safe in this environment.

I decide though, a makeover is needed, it seems a good plan to redecorate and let the boys update their rooms. Some change is therapeutic, it also allows us to move forward and make new memories as we go.

Some decorators are recommended to me and I invite them to the house to see what needs doing. The guys seem really nice - one is very chatty; the other is quiet and looks sad. I feel comfortable with them in the house and agree for the work to start.

Within a few days of them starting work Oliver seems like a different child. He is not sat in front of the television when I get home from work. Instead he is bombarding me with information about scuba diving, sharks and stone fish. I listen to him and suddenly I start to see my inquisitive chatty little boy returning. It becomes obvious that he has talked non-stop to the team of decorators and that he has really enjoyed their company. He shows me some photographs of sharks and then he shows me a shark's tooth. "Look what Phil has given me?", he is so, so excited.

I speak to Phil and thank him for his kindness - Phil is the quieter of the two men. He smiles for the first time and says it is a pleasure and that scuba diving is a passion of his and that he is an underwater photographer - I like him.

Oliver really seems to blossom during the time the decorators are with us and he is sad again when the first section of work is completed, and they leave. They promise to come back soon. I am surprised, but I miss the chatter too!

I make the decision to take Oliver for a Dyslexia assessment at the recognised centre in Coventry. It is the same centre I had taken Anthony to when he was fourteen. Oliver is almost nine and I think now is the time to address his problems.

Like Anthony, I am told that Oliver is extremely dyslexic with a very high IQ, he is also suffering with dyspraxia. I know his coordination is not great, he is terrible at eye to ball contact. In fact, his biggest sporting strength is swimming. He has always been able to swim like a fish underwater and Tony would take him regularly. I am not such a good swimmer.

I address the report with the school and I request for a statement of special needs be put into place. I have the report, and this is sent off to Solihull Borough Council.

A Statement of Special Needs is a formal document detailing a child's learning difficulties and the help they will be given. The first stage is a statutory assessment which is carried out by the local authority. This is a detailed exploration into a child's learning needs. The school or a parent can ask for a statutory assessment. The local authority has six to twelve weeks to decide whether to go ahead.

Meanwhile, Phil has become a regular visitor at the house. He regales Oliver with stories of underwater diving and ship wrecks and Oliver is completely fascinated. I definitely look forward to his visits. I discover that my initial observation of Phil being sad was correct and that he has recently divorced. He is so patient with Oliver I am surprised that he does not have any children of his own.

I really want to build on Oliver's confidence and decide to work on his strengths, the main one being his love of swimming and water. This seems like a good plan but in order to achieve it I need to get over my own fear of water. So, without anyone knowing, I go along to 'Scooba Boosta' in Warwick and decide to learn to scuba dive! I know that Oliver would be a natural, but in order for him to qualify as a PADI Junior, he will need to do a written exam confirming his understanding of the physics and dangers.

I am good at the classroom side of things, I am not however, so confident underwater in a swimming pool. Everyone knows I swim with my head well out of the water and I really hate getting water in my eyes; this is going to be a major challenge for me. Learning to clear a mask underwater is my first nightmare, followed by clearing my regulator. There is an awful lot of spluttering and complaining, but after six weeks I have completed the written exam and can remove my whole diving kit underwater and put it back on again - result.

The final part of learning to dive will be in open water.

It is now time to share my news with the world. Oliver is over the moon and suitably impressed by my achievement especially when he learns he will start the same course next week.

Phil is also impressed, and we decide to book a holiday to Egypt for both Oliver and I to complete our Open Water exams. Oliver is ecstatic!

As I thought, the pool side of things was a doddle for him, and the classroom side was more difficult because of his ability to read. I read each chapter with him and explain anything he is unsure of, he answers all the questions and is a quick learner. His understanding levels are remarkable for a boy of his age. The questions are read to him in the exam and thankfully he passes first time. Open water here we come!

At the school governors meeting, I am outraged to see the response from Solihull Council. They obviously did not realise that as a Governor I would get to see their response. Oliver's needs are not great enough in their opinion!

I am straight on the phone to the local authority. I ask whether they had bothered to read the independent report that had been sent, and could they explain to me on what basis they did not value Oliver's needs great enough. They could not explain their decision.

I then begin to explain in detail the problems my son has overcome, the fact that he has just passed a scuba diving exam that most adults would find difficult and the fact he has an extremely high IQ. He is desperate to learn and at the moment he is not being given the help or support he requires. If this continues, he will lose all interest in school and this will be their fault. If this happens, I will personally hold the authority responsible and I will sue for damages. Wow, I'm really not sure where that came from, but I will fight for my sons no matter what. That hidden strength certainly shows itself when required.

There was silence for a moment and then an apology and an acknowledgment that they would like to meet Oliver. I tell them they can visit him at home or at school. They decide to meet him at school.

A week later I receive a call from the local authorities explaining that they have met with Oliver and they are overwhelmed by his knowledge, his interests and his maturity. They confirm a statement will be in place for next term to assist and prepare him for secondary school a year later.

As I take control of my life, several friends are in need of comfort, Gill who rushed to my aid following Tony's death, now has to deal with the sudden death of her husband whilst he is in Trinidad, leaving her and her two young sons in despair.

Oliver's Godfather, Franco, who is Italian, is seriously injured in a car accident, subsequently dying from his injuries and leaving my oldest friend Alison a widow - also at the age of 38 - life can be so cruel.

My dear friend Patty, who was the provider of so, so many meals for our family following Tony's death is now nursing her beloved husband Bill through terminal cancer. Heart breaking!

It is now time to pay back the love and support offered to me and my family in our hour of need.

Chapter 10
Happier Times

We have no choice but to move on in life. For me the happy times are also the saddest times. The times I remember what Tony is missing out on.

The birth of his first Grandchild Indira, following Tony's death, is one of these times. Helen's pregnancy has not been easy, her health had certainly suffered. So, it is with great relief when the baby is eventually born, and Mother and baby are fine.

Our family get togethers in London at Christmas or at a Christening or birthday celebrations are always special.

Victoria is following her dream in Australia and Gerard is thriving with his new job. So much to be grateful for.

Anthony has completed his A 'levels and is off to University. At first, he told me he wanted to stay local - I knew it was because he was worried about leaving us. I told him that this was really not necessary. So, he has decided on Plymouth! I am happy, particularly because his friend John is also going to Plymouth, it may be 200 miles door to door, but they will take care of each other. He is also now eighteen, another milestone.

Oliver has mastered scuba diving and is a star, he has even been awarded a Blue Peter Badge for his hard work.

Phil is a big part of our lives now and is very supportive to us all, he even has Mum under his spell.

Tony is never far from my thoughts and as a family we have donated a Tony McAtamney Cup which will be presented at the Law Society Championship in June, three years on from Tony's death. It is really important for me to take Oliver with me so that he can have some closure on where his Daddy died. Anthony is also looking forward to the holiday.

As we arrive in Novo Sancti Petri, I reflect on how different I feel three years on. I can smile again, and I can feel happy. We are greeted by the legal teams from all over the world including Canada, England & Ireland. It is wonderful to watch the boy's swimming in the pools and jumping waves in the sea. It is with great pride that we present the cup to the Irish team, very poignant considering Tony's background, he would have approved. The cup will travel to Ireland until it is returned in three years' time.

As time moves on, I have a lot to be thankful for. I continue to work around the boys and they are thriving. After a lot of nagging we have a new member joining our family, his name is Monty and he is Oliver's dog.

Even after all this time Oliver is still uncertain about sleeping in the dark. He has nagged and nagged about getting a dog and so I give in and we take a trip to the Dogs Trust.

Phil is with us and Oliver's friend Callum. We wander through the kennels looking at the different dogs, some are big, others small and others extremely noisy. We look in one kennel at the very end where an enormous dog is sat. He looks very sad and he is drooling he does not want to engage with us. He looks like a cross between a Labrador and a Saint Bernard. He is very nice and big!

We sit with the kennel assistants and discuss the dogs we like. It seems there are not many suitable for our home. "What about the big one?", Oliver won't be ignored, and the lady suddenly smiles, "oh yes, he would be fine. Do you want to walk him in the grounds?".

We wait outside and are greeted by the most beautiful creature; his tail is wagging and his golden coat shimmering in the sunshine. He is gorgeous. The assistant passes me the dog lead and I am smitten. I drop to the floor and look him in the eyes, we connect immediately. I know he is big, but he is also beautiful and well behaved on the lead. Oliver takes him for a walk.

As we return to the kennels a couple tap me on the shoulder, "Are you having that dog?", without hesitation I find myself clutching the lead and telling them, "yes, most certainly."

Oliver and Callum are leaping around with excitement and Phil looks at me and asks if I am sure. Strangely enough I have never been surer about anything in my life. I have an immediate bond with this dog.

The kennel assistant is astonished and explains that Monty has been with them for 6 months and in all of that time no one had chosen to take him out for a walk. It was as if Monty had been invisible inside the kennel. Apparently, he was obese when he arrived, he had been born in the Dog's Trust and then returned to them when his owners had a baby and lost interest in him. They had had him five and a half years, how cruel. No wonder he looks so sad.

How strange that as soon as we take him out for a walk someone else is also interested. Well they are not having him because we are!

It is also explained that they will need to inspect the house and garden, and also Mum and Anthony will need to come and meet Monty to make sure that they get on.

Anthony loves him immediately, but Mum is a bit scared, she thinks he is a small horse. By the time we leave the Dogs Trust everyone is happy with the arrangement. The young man who visits the house and garden gives us 10 out of 10 and asks if he can move in too!

Anthony drives us to collect Monty, he has been showered and is still wet. He seems really excited to be leaving the kennels. He climbs on the back seat of the car with Oliver and he looks almost as big as Oliver. Oliver seems more than happy to have a large wet dog sat on him so off we leave for home.

Mum is waiting at the front door. Monty does not hesitate, he runs straight past her through the patio doors and into our garden. He is running around the garden like a mad thing, only stopping to glance into the pond. It appears he has never seen fish before. He is home.

We break all the rules and allow Monty to explore upstairs. He seems more than impressed with his sofa bed situated in Oliver's bedroom. We are all astonished when for the first time since Tony's death, Oliver goes to bed, switches his bedside lamp off and closes the door.

All is going well, Oliver at 12 is more than capable of walking Monty and seems really happy to do so. I take him to the vets for a check-up and advice on diet and care. The vet confirms that he is in good shape but still needs to lose some weight and we are all happy to help achieve this by lots of walks.

As I sit having a cup of coffee, I read through Monty's information pack and records. I almost choke as I stare at his date of birth, 28th June 2004. The date screams out at me, Monty was born in the Dogs Trust on the very day Tony died! So weird, I have goose bumps! I call my friend immediately who analyses the situation even further. "My goodness, have you done the anagram of Monty? its TonyM! It was obviously meant to be as Monty fits into life at Patrick House like a glove.

It is hard to believe that life is progressing so quickly. Anthony has finished University in Plymouth and has his degree in Computer Science, about to start work. Oliver is thriving at secondary school with the help of his statement. I am delighted by his yearly reports and achievements, he has received special achievement awards in many subjects including English, History and Religious Studies which considering that he is dyslexic is pretty amazing. He is an Explorer in the scouts and plays Rugby for the local team. I am particularly amazed by his foreign studies and visits, he has spent many exchange trips to Germany and France and has made many friends along the way.

I am continuing to run the recruitment agency and the best pleasure I get from this is helping people find their ideal job. Sometimes they have been ill or bullied in previous employment and are suffering loss of confidence. I see in them the look I once had; of desperation, of feeling that everything is impossible, and it gives me great satisfaction to show them that everything is possible and that they can get the job of their dreams.

I am finding myself out and about more, doing locum work as a legal cashier. It is one area of employment where I struggle to get replacement staff and so quite often I do it myself. I have to admit, it is also nice working as part of an office team as sometimes recruitment can be quite lonely. The best of both worlds.

I am also still fundraising, my favourite hobby! I helped to raise around £30,000 at Berkswell School during the time I was joint chair, and I have chaired the Heart of England PTA for several years arranging Prom Fairs, Balls and Christmas Fairs. It really does feel good to give back!

Chapter 11
My Accident

I can hardly believe that Oliver is now fifteen and revising for his GCSE's at the Heart of England School. Anthony is working doing a job he loves, and Mum is still going to keep fit twice a week and looks incredible for a lady of seventy-six. Monty is still trying to lose weight, he is definitely fit, but his love of food makes it impossible not to spoil him. Mum has made a compromise and now gives him tuna for lunch and not a sausage!

A firm I have worked for on many occasions has offered me a permanent part time position within their accounts department as an assistant cashier. This actually works quite well for me as I know all the staff and like the office. It also allows me to be around Oliver whilst he is studying, just in case he needs some support. I work five hours a day and still keep my hand in with the recruitment business.

Phil is working away at the moment and it is bitterly cold with snow on the ground. I cannot complain as it is February. Friday 22nd February, a day I will remember for a long time.

I arrive at work as usual and head up the three flights of stairs to the office I share with Naomi. It is unusually quiet for a Friday, no completions. I make a coffee and glance at the pile of paperwork to be returned to the archive room. It is not a nice job, but it is part of what I have to do. I tell Naomi where I am going and disappear into the freezing cold basement.

I should have kept my coat on as it really is cold. The only daylight I can see is the pavement where the snow is settling above my head. The room is dark, gloomy, smelly and covered in cobwebs. The files are crammed everywhere, and it is hard to get your fingers between them. Some are very heavy and bulky. I climb the rickety old ladders left for me to use to try and reach the top shelf. It is a bit of a struggle but using both hands I try and retrieve a file from the top shelf. I tug and tug and then all of a sudden, several of the files come loose and completely knock me off balance. I am juggling with the files in the air and trying to save myself, but the last thing I know is that I am hitting the floor in a superman fashion, arms still outstretched. I am aware of files falling on top of me and the ladders. Then blackness.

I know something is badly wrong. I am shaking uncontrollably on the freezing cold stone floor, I am finding it difficult to breathe from the pain in the side of my chest and I cannot lift my arm which my head is lying on.

I know I am in trouble. It is no good shouting as no one will hear. I struggle to move my left arm and manage to lift my mobile phone from my pocket. It is all too painful. I cannot stop shaking and I feel like I want to sleep. With my left hand I manage to hit Naomi's number. I know she has answered but I'm not sure what I am saying. I think I am muttering the word "fallen" and then darkness.

There is now commotion going on around me. It hurts too much, and I just want to sleep. I am shaking violently. People are calling my name and trying to wake me. I am unable to move. Coats are being draped over me and people are trying to squeeze around me but there is no room amongst the rows of files.

Gradually I begin to come around and I feel really embarrassed. The ladies around me are lovely and trying to comfort and keep me warm. An ambulance has been called. I keep apologising and then I think I'm going to be sick. The ambulance arrives, and I thank the ladies for their kindness.

The ambulance crew mutter about how "grim" the archiving room is, comparing it to something out of Dickens. They quickly start to try and move me as the room is so cold. They manage to get my shoulder over my head and I am helped to my feet. I can hardly breathe. With their assistance I am able to walk to the ambulance thankfully as a stretcher would have been near on impossible.

In the ambulance I am wrapped in blankets to heat me up and then I am checked over. The crew are lovely. They don't think my shoulder is broken but they are not sure about my ribs. They think I am probably suffering from cold and shock. I am given some painkillers to help ease the pain and they decide it probably is a good idea for me to be checked over at the hospital.

Naomi accompanies me in the ambulance and tells me how shocked she was when she found me on the floor unconscious. I think the impact of hitting the concrete winded me. Thank goodness it was not my head that hit the floor. My head and neck thankfully had bounced onto my shoulder. It was my shoulder and ribs that took the full impact. She said everyone was looking for the first aider - and I was on the floor!

I am sick again in the ambulance and I am relieved when we arrive at Warwick Hospital. I do not want Naomi to call my Mum, Anthony or Oliver, I don't want them worried. I am the walking wounded and still shaking uncontrollably. I try and see the funny side to cover my embarrassment, but it hurts to laugh.

Naomi insists on calling Anthony as I am called in to see a Doctor who examines me and takes me to x-ray. I feel like I am in a dream, everything hurts especially breathing. She wraps me in a blanket to control the shaking. She tells me that I have a rotator cuff injury. I ask if that is something like a dislocation and I think she agrees, although my head is feeling really muzzy. She tells me I have a chest injury and that the hospital does not treat broken or bruised ribs. She tells me to take plenty of pain relief and she hands me some ibuprofen. I am told if my breathing gets worse to come back to the hospital or my GP. I am not really taking this in - I want to go home.

I am then discharged and find Anthony waiting with Naomi. He gives me a careful hug, frightened he might hurt me. I struggle with the seatbelt and we drop Naomi back at work and head home.

Oliver is really cross that no one has informed him. But he is relieved to see I am okay. Mum is almost hysterical when she finds out. Of course, the memory of my Dad breaking his neck from a fall yet again raises its ugly head.

My sister takes charge and it suddenly dawns on me all the things I am unable to do. I am completely mentally exhausted and now the pain killers are wearing off I am in a lot of pain.

I cannot get comfortable, sitting, standing or in bed. I cannot undress, get dressed or shower. I cannot wash my hair, dry my hair and definitely not straighten my hair. I am unable to walk very far, and I feel constantly sick from the pain killers and looking at the growing black bruises on my body. I am frustrated, hurt, angry and extremely tired.

I have never been reliant on other people to take care of me and now here I am unable to do anything for myself. I have never had time off work, even after the birth of my children. I have never not been able to drive. I feel completely isolated and vulnerable. Phil is due home from Barcelona in a couple of days and I refuse to allow him to come home earlier. I do not want people seeing me in this state.

Every time I fall asleep, I wake in a panic either trying to stop myself from falling and juggling files in the air or being back on that dark, cold concrete floor. Then the what if's set in. What if nobody had found me on that floor, I could have been there for hours. What if I had hit my head? My heart is pounding, I cannot be having a panic attack!

The boys, Mum and Tina are brilliant and are doing absolutely everything for me. I am not a good patient and I feel pathetic! Phil arrives home and is completely shocked! "You said you were okay, just look at you, you are black and blue, you look like you have been beaten". This is not good - Phil is angry because I should have told him the extent of my injuries. I know how I look - I have also been sick from the tablets and I look frail. I am not good at asking for help. I feel like my life is out of control again and I am terrified that I won't cope.

After several weeks of increased pain management, physio, injections in my shoulder and rest I am slowly on the mend. I am able to, dress myself but doing my hair is a nightmare. Cooking is still out of the question and I can barely lift a kettle. My confidence is shattered, and this is not helped by the behaviour of the partners at the office where I work - they have not been very nice.

I now know I will not be returning to the office - I do feel really let down by people I believed to be professionals and people I liked and trusted and even thought were friends. It is another lesson in life not to be so gullible. I will not let this accident destroy me, and as soon as I can drive again, I will look for work. I will not be a victim. I will certainly not let my boys see how badly I have been affected. Oliver is about to do his exams and I will let nothing get in the way of him succeeding.

Sadly, I am unable to go to Lourdes in April this year with the St. Bernadette Trust, something I have done each year since Tony's death and having taken his place as a Trustee. Over the years, it has given me great strength to see how people with chronic illnesses and disabilities can be so resilient and enjoy life to the full. Pushing wheelchairs and holding the hands of sick children is both humbling and rewarding. My recent injuries are nothing to what some of these people have to deal with - I stop feeling sorry for myself immediately!

The gym is a no, no! This makes me cross as prior to the accident I would go four or five times a week and do Body Pump, Body Conditioning and Spin. Now the thought of even raising my hand over my head makes me feel sick! Walking the dog is just about possible - he does not pull and although I still get a bit breathless - the exercise is lovely.

Anthony has taken over most of the running around in the car taking Oliver to and from scouts, rugby and friends. Between them, they are all doing the shopping and house work. I am very fortunate.

After six weeks I can drive at last. I know I still have a long road to fully recover and I will do everything I can to regain my fitness. I am still taking nightly pain relief and sleeping is an issue, but I am ready to return to working life as soon as I can.

Almost immediately I get the call to do some locum cover and accept at once. I am very nervous about returning to work but after the first day my confidence is back. I have a firm of Solicitors who are desperate for some help in their accounts department. I can find no one experienced enough through my agency, so against my better judgement take on the position myself.

I throw myself into full time work, and soon have things under control in the office and I am starting to feel more in control of my life. I am still undergoing physio and Mum does my hair in the morning before I go to work as I can still not use the straighteners! She is also still doing a lot of the cooking, hanging out washing and general house work whilst I am working. She is a gem.

My family are the most important thing in the world to me and if they are happy and well, then I have everything.

Chapter 12
Coping with illness

So, life goes on and the boys are doing well. Oliver has been made Head Boy at School, yet again I am oozing with pride.

I am continuing to work full time, but Mum is not well. Her health has not been good for some time. Her Doctor keeps telling us that she is stressed and not to worry. With that diagnosis in mind my sister and I take the boys away to Turkey on holiday for a week. My Niece Natasha is watching over Nan. Tom and Oliver had a fantastic holiday, but both my sister and I knew deep down Mum was not right.

Our worst fears were confirmed when we arrived home. Mum looked terrible. Her stomach had swollen as if she was expecting twins and her arms and legs were skeleton thin. How could this have happened in a week?

I rush Mum to hospital completely missing out the doctors. We see a Specialist who does a scan and we are called in to see him. He is a lovely man, with a booming voice and big smile. He calls us back into the room, I am rubbing my shoulder, the more stress I have, the more my shoulder hurts. But this is not about me. Within minutes the words I have been dreading are out. "Well Shirl, you have cancer", I can feel my world turn upside down. I become very aware that Mum is not saying anything, she is just watching me. I know she needs me to be strong. I gather all my hidden strength, which I had used not to cry when Tony died. Calmly, I ask what happens next; the door opens and in enters a Macmillan Nurse.

We learn that Mum has inoperable stage four ovarian and stomach cancer, her stomach will need to be drained and they will then see how strong she is, if she is strong enough to have chemotherapy. The words are swimming around my brain - cancer - chemotherapy - Macmillan Nurses - my Mum is going to die!

I put my most positive voice on and tell Mum that all will be fine. Mum will be admitted in two days. I tell my sister as I walk, to get the car - we are both in bits. I get back to Mum and continue to tell her everything will be okay. She is still very quiet. I actually think she is relieved; I think she thought she was going mad. At last people believe her, she is ill.

Arriving home, the boys are amazing. This is the first near death situation we have had since Tony's death. They hug Nan and tell her that she will be okay and that we will all take care of her. I walk Monty and cry my eyes out!

Mum's condition deteriorates overnight and she is rushed into hospital. The Macmillan nurse meets me and confirms that Mum is very sick and that they need to drain her stomach as soon as possible. They are not sure whether she will come through. I am to tell all the family. She is put in a room on her own and we are told that because of the seriousness of her condition visitors can come at any time. We should prepare ourselves for the worst.

I leave the hospital and go into work. I tell the partners the position and that I will need to reduce my hours 'if' Mum comes through the operation. I will need to be with her for recovery and chemotherapy. I am not impressed by their response, "Can someone else not do it?", I explain very firmly, even if someone else could do it, I would be the one doing it!

Mum survives surgery, but she is very poorly.

I go into work the next morning, I am a bit late, because I have forgotten to pick up a birthday card for one of the partners. It is a silly tradition, but the Practice Manager, which is me, has to get a card for staff birthdays and everyone signs it. Last thing on my mind really but I do it anyway. I walk into my office. I am completely shocked when I come under attack for being late - from the partner whose birthday card I have been to buy. "As you have chosen to work part time - the least you can do is turn up on time!".

Enough is enough, I pick up my coat and walk out. I burst into tears in the car and decide I do not like Lawyers!

I cannot deal with work, my Mum needs to come first. I leave a telephone message to say I will not be back until my Mum's condition has improved. I see my GP who confirms that I am not fit for work anyway - I need to take some time out.

With this decided, I concentrate on how best to help Mum. It is her birthday tomorrow and she will be seventy-nine. How do I deal with this? The Macmillan Nurses do not believe she will recover. She is not eating and seems to have lost hope. How do you celebrate? I pinch myself, where there is life, there is hope. I get myself to the florist and order the biggest balloon bouquet they can make. I almost float into the hospital and I take a deep breath before opening the door to Mum's room. She is sleeping and looks very pale but as she hears me come in her eyes open and she smiles immediately at the sight of the balloons. They fill the corner of the room. They certainly seem to have lifted her spirit.

I hold Mum's hand and whisper "Happy Birthday Darling". We sit and talk; she wants to come home. I explain that she cannot come home unless she starts to eat again to build up her strength. I know from the talks with the nurses that she will not be offered chemotherapy if she does not get stronger. She will have to walk in to see the oncologist unaided, and at the moment she cannot stand by herself. Deep down I am terrified of Mum having chemotherapy, I don't want to see her get sicker and to lose her hair, but equally I am not ready to lose her. "Mum, you need to fight this, I know there is no cure for your cancer but if you get strong enough to have chemo it can be managed". Bless her, I see that spark in her eyes, "I want to try".

The family come in and out and we all start to tempt Mum with whatever she fancies, even the specialist comes in and offers her a chocolate ēclair, "Come on Shirl, eat this up, I am too fat and would love to eat it, chocolate eclairs are my favourite cakes". Mum takes a bite.

I am due to visit University with Oliver, thankfully my friend Karen is driving. Oliver has his heart set on the University of Nottingham, he will need to work really hard to make the grades, but he wants it. Karen's son Edward is pretty keen too. It would be lovely if they both go together as they have been friends since nursery.

I am in a daze as we wander around the University. It looks fantastic and I know it would be perfect for Oliver. I switch off every now and then and take in the surroundings and then I feel the sadness overcome me. This is all about Oliver's future, Mum probably does not have a future and so will not be able to share it with him. Times like this I still miss Tony so much. I shake the sadness off and I am happy for Oliver. He cannot wait to tell Nan all about it when he gets back. We go straight to the hospital and he tells her all the news. She is happy for him.

I talk to Tina and we decide to ask if Mum can come home. The Macmillan Nurse thinks it is a good idea, we should spend quality time with Mum. She still does not think she will be strong enough for chemo and she thinks that we should make the most of the time left. I have other ideas.

Mum is discharged, and we are given an appointment to see the oncologist in two weeks' time. I start by making Mum drink the build-up milk shakes - she seems to like these. I give her two a day. Oliver takes her tea every hour and we make tiny meals every two hours. She starts to get stronger. We continue to feed her cake, sweet fizzy drinks and anything she fancies.

None of Mum's clothes fit her, they are all hanging off her. This is not a good look. I go shopping and buy her new clothes, bright and comfortable and a new lip-stick, very important!

On the day of Mum's appointment, she comes downstairs and she looks amazing. She has make-up on and is wearing her new clothes and lip-stick. She holds my arm as we walk from the hospital car park and she is looking confident, she wants this!

Mum's name is called and she gets up and marches towards the oncologist's room, I follow behind. As the door opens, I realise the Macmillan Nurse is also in the room. I see the look of shock on her face as she sees Mum. She looks at me with a beaming smile.

The Oncologist has never met Mum so does not know what the fuss is about. He starts to talk to Mum and tell her about the chemotherapy treatment on offer. He looks at me and asks if I have any questions. I convey my worries about Mum's age, her losing her hair and whether it will make her sick. I am quickly reassured that Mum's age is not a concern and that many ladies of Mum's age are successfully treated with this form of chemotherapy, she will not lose her hair and apart from being tired, it should not make her feel ill.

I am relieved and optimistic. Mum looks happy and confirms immediately that she wants to proceed with the treatment. The Nurse takes me aside and congratulates me on getting Mum back on her feet. I laugh and tell her that it is nothing to do with me, Mum is an amazing lady.

The Nurse is great and offers to sort out a Blue Badge for Mum and to sort out some extra funding to help pay for new clothing etc. She is so helpful, I know nothing about benefits and I am happy for someone else to deal with this. We leave the room and my sister is waiting outside, she is nervous about what has happened. She is delighted to know Mum has been given a chance of treatment.

I return to work on a part-time basis. I make sure Mum is up and dressed in the morning and has had her breakfast before I leave. I know that nurses and friends will call in throughout the morning. Mum also starts to have another visitor, Father Frank Smith, the new parish priest. The more Mum sees of Father Frank the more she seems to be coming to terms with her illness and prognosis. I begin to see a real positive change both mentally and physically. I am not sure where Father Frank has come from, but his timing is wonderful, and I will be forever grateful.

Chemo day has arrived, I am terrified and feel sick, Mum seems quite excited. We enter the incredible world of chemotherapy, I look around the ward and there are about 20 chairs with people attached to machines. Cancer certainly attacks everyone, young, old, black, white, short and tall people. The one thing in common is how supportive the patients are towards each other. The nurses put Mum's arm in a bucket of warm water to enable them to find a vein to fit the canula. My stomach flips and I have to leave the room, pathetic, Mum is comforting me! I sit and watch as Mum is pumped full of the toxic looking substance. She is coping well and chatting to everyone; I am quiet. The nurses come around with sandwiches and I am amazed when Mum tucks into hers. They offer me some lunch and I shake my head. I cannot hold coffee down even. My shoulder is aching as I sit in the chair and I rub it for comfort. Stress always makes it worse.

We go home with a bag of follow up pills and potions and a red book full of side effects to look out for. I am nervous, but Mum seems fine. I have a bowl in the car, but she does not feel sick, although I do! Mum copes really well and true to the Oncologist's word the only side effect is tiredness. By the time Mum has her first set of blood tests in December she is looking and feeling really well. The results are staggering, the cancer has reduced in size and she now has the option of surgery.

We have a good Christmas and return to the hospital in January. It is really strange, we have been really excited that Mum has been offered surgery. It suddenly dawns on me as I sit listening to the doctor speak to Mum, that this is major. Mum has never had surgery in her life, she is in her 80th year. We are sent for pre-ops and I suddenly ask Mum, "Do you want this?" she answers immediately and says, no, she had thought that I wanted her to have it! I immediately get up and tell the staff that Mum has changed her mind. We leave the hospital.

The church and Father Frank have become a great strength and comfort to Mum. I arrive home from work and she tells me she has decided to convert, she is becoming a Catholic. I am delighted for her. Mum has always attended church but had never taken the step to convert. I am very proud of Mum, she is very strong minded and at seventy-nine she is still making her own decisions in life.

The NHS are amazing. They do not give up on Mum after she refuses surgery, instead they offer her the opportunity to take part in a drugs trial. We get to meet the incredible Professor Poole. At our first appointment he examines Mum and tells her that she is in 'good nick' for a lady of her years and apart from having cancer she is as fit as a fiddle. So, the cancer trials begin.

There are not many families lucky enough not to be touched by cancer, the uncertainty, the rollercoaster of good and bad news and heartache of watching someone you love suffer. Feeling helpless, I decide to set up a fundraising page and support Race for Life 10K. I have done the 5k some years ago and it was a doddle. Our page is set up for 'Team Shirley' and the money starts to roll in. Unfortunately, I did not appreciate that since my accident I am unable to run! Silly really, I hadn't given it a thought but once training starts, I know running is out of the question. Power walking also hurts but this is nothing to my Mum's suffering, I head to the doctors and a very sympathetic doctor gives me some extra strong painkillers, tells me not to drive whilst taking them, but that they will get me through the race. She also recommends further physiotherapy on my shoulder. I know this will help but at the moment my time is taken up with Mum's hospital visits, work would really not be impressed if I ask for more time off for physio.

Team Shirley runs the Race for Life apart from me, who walks it! As I take Mum for more chemo in the cancer trial unit every bone in my body hurts from the 10K walk, I am offered a seat and explain that it is too painful to sit down. No gain without pain!

Amidst Mum's treatment Oliver is taking his A 'level exams. I don't think I have ever been so proud of him, he has spent the last year raising money for a Memory Garden for the Sixth Form, it is following the sudden death of a fellow student who died in her sleep. Her death happened at the end of first year sixth form, Oliver was Deputy Head boy and it was part of his duty to do the end of term speech to the rest of the school. It was harrowing, he had called me at work - having prepared his speech, he had arrived at school to hear the devasting news that this poor girl had died. The staff, parents and students were understandably devastated. I just cried on the end of the phone. Oliver told me he had rewritten his speech, and would I listen; it was an absolute tribute to the girl. He talked about over the years, how in the assembly students are told, year after year, that they would need to stand out from the crowd. He said Ella did! He went on to talk about her achievements in her short lifetime and how she would be remembered for them. I cried more and apparently so did the rest of the school, but he did it, he completed his speech - I'm not sure I could have! He had come a long way from the seven-year-old who lost his Daddy.

Mum has also become a day patient at the Marie Curie Hospice in Solihull. The Macmillan Nurses had suggested it might help Mum and that it would give me some respite once a week. At first, she hated the idea, Hospices are places where people go to die. True, but I tried to explain that they are also places where people learn to live whilst they are dying. I pleaded with her to give it a go and if she didn't like it, she did not have to go again.

I wait in trepidation as a car pulls up to collect Mum. She is still not happy, but she is going to give it a try. The doorbell rings and a gentleman is stood waiting to escort Mum to his Jaguar. She looks suitably impressed. He introduces himself as Gilbert and she takes his arm and doesn't look back. It is like sending a child to first day at school, rather than respite I do not know what to do with myself. What if she hates it?

At 5.00pm she arrives home with Gilbert, he walks her to the door and gives her a kiss on her cheek, she is smitten. She proceeds to tell me about Gilbert who is a volunteer, who had lost his wife to cancer. She talks about the nurses and the other patients. She enjoyed lunch, painting and relaxation! Monday soon becomes a cherished day for Mum.

On exam results day, Oliver and I are up at 6.00am. I have not slept all night. What if he does not get his results? What if he is not accepted at Nottingham? I suddenly hear a commotion in the study, the door flies open, and he swings me around. He has his results and he has his place at University. I am so happy for him. Daddy would have been so happy for him.

I am concerned about Mum, she is very feverish and rather than her temperature being high, it is low. I ring the hospital and they tell me to bring her to the ward immediately. We get to hospital as fast as we can, with Mum protesting all the way that she is okay. It is confirmed immediately that she is not okay, she has sepsis.

Mum has now been in hospital for two weeks. Apparently, the infection was started by an ingrown toe nail. I had asked a nurse to check her toe and was told it was fine. It obviously wasn't, and Professor Poole confirmed that this is definitely the cause. She is getting better, but her bloods are still not right.

I am thrown into a complete panic. Mum is eighty at the end of the week. I have organised a meal at a hotel for forty friends and family. I speak to Professor Poole and explain my concern. I know the risk for Mum. But I also know this is probably the last time she will see all these people who care about her. The next time they are together may well be her funeral. He is completely understanding and tells me he will discharge her and that I can bring her straight back if she is ill.

My hunch pays off and the party is the perfect medicine she needs. She has a lovely evening with friends and family and she looks like a princess all dressed up. She is stable for now.

The day has come to take Oliver to University. I am in bits, what is wrong with me? Phil packs the car and Oliver hugs Nan, she is crying. We get to Nottingham and have an hour slot to park, unload and say our goodbyes. Oliver knows no one in his halls. He seems quite happy, just a bit nervous, but happy. I cry the whole way home. Phil looks at me as if I am mad, "for goodness sake, you have left him at University not prison", the sobs continue!

News at the hospital is not good, and Mum is taken off the trial, it is not working for her. We have an appointment to see Professor Poole in January, but it seems they are just leaving her for the time being.

It is strange, but her health seems to be improving. I take her to visit Oliver at University so that she can visualise where he is and not worry about him. We take him out to lunch. I take Mum up to his room in Halls, he panics about the risk of germs and infection. I reassure him that Nan is off chemo at the moment and that she will be fine. He looks uneasy at this response and asks why they have stopped the chemo. I answer him truthfully as it is the only way with Oliver. We have a lovely day and head back home. Mum cries again.

I know that at some point I will need to finish work to help support Mum through her final stages of cancer. I don't ever want her to think that this is a chore, it really isn't, it is what any daughter would do. Mum knows my passion has always been event planning and fundraising, I am already working with 53RD Scout Group in Berkswell to help their fundraising appeal to build a new Scout House. A Ball is planned for November and I tell Mum all about the plans and persuade her that she must come. Like me, Mum has always loved the romance of music, dancing and dressing up like a princess. I pray she will be well enough to attend.

There are over 200 people attending the Ball and Mum is well enough to attend. The event is a big success, thanks especially to the lovey Joanne Malin who hosts the evening. Mum manages to stay until after the meal and then begins to look tired and is taken home. She has had a great evening, sadly I think, probably one of her last. £7000 is raised and a great start for the new build, the scouts are happy!

I start to make further plans for events and know it will be my way forward when the time is right.

Before we know where we are it is Christmas again and Mum is looking really well. The MacMillan Nurse visits us at home and is shocked at how well Mum looks. She makes me promise to insist on seeing Professor Poole at the next appointment, not his Registrar. She believes Mum may be strong enough for further treatment.

At her appointment, she is called to see the Registrar. I stand my ground and explain that I wish her to be seen by Professor Poole. We wait a bit longer and we are called in to see Professor Poole, he is not cross, just amazed at how well Mum looks. He immediately assigns her to a new cancer treatment programme.

All seems well until April; Mum's bloods are not showing an improvement. Professor Poole tells Mum he needs to change her treatment to a more aggressive form of chemotherapy. She asks whether she will lose her hair and whether she will be sick. He replies yes to both; I am trying not to cry. Mum smiles at Professor Poole and tells him she would like to finish treatment. She tells him that when she dies, she wants to die with her hair. She is not frightened of dying. I cannot stop the tears running down my cheeks. This is her decision and it is the right one.

She is very brave and asks Professor Poole what happens next. He explains that she will be passed over to Palliative Care and as she is already attending Marie Curies Hospice, they will take over her care. He tells us that she may well have an Indian Summer! Professor Poole tries once more to change Mum's mind, but her mind is made up.

I know it is now time for me to finish work to be with Mum full time. It has worked out well for leaving work as it is the end of year and a replacement has been found for me. I will miss the girls at the office, but I can leave guilt free. As well as planning events my sensible head has taken over and I have managed to find a flexible self-employed legal cashier position in Stratford-upon-Avon, just fifteen hours a week, Bonell & Co are lovely. The move feels right and they are immediately supportive - it is really strange how things happen at the right time.

Mum is really having more bad days than good; her morphine is being increased and it is an emotional time for me and my sister. We do our best to take Mum out when she is well and sit with her at home when she is not so good. She still enjoys mass on Sunday and is able to walk the short distance holding my arm to get there. I feel time is running out.

Chapter 13
Saying Goodbye

Mum is trying to put a brave face on things but managing the pain is becoming more difficult to control. I am hosting a charity afternoon tea at home to raise funds for the parish church. In hindsight this is probably not the best plan but it is organised now and it will happen. My great fundraising friend Anne is on the case with me and the garden is looking stunning. My sister is busy trying to get Mum ready, she is really not good today.

As the guests arrive, I get on with the job at hand. I am delighted to see Mum appear in the garden, she has her lipstick on and she is smiling, the world does not know the pain behind that mask, but I do. Of course, Mum's afternoon is made perfect by the arrival of Father Frank, she is happy. I know the illness is moving to a new level.

Mum's brother arrives from America with his wife Renee and their twin daughters Rebecca and Nicole. Ben has always been able to make Mum smile. The cancer is taking hold, the morphine is no longer working. I can no longer bare to see

Mum in such pain. I break down to Ben and Renee, we need help. I know what I need to do, and I get on the telephone to the Hospice, I am tearful and tell them Mum needs help to manage the pain.

The Hospice is fantastic, and they tell me to pack a bag for Mum to be admitted for a few days. She is happy to go. I laugh at her because she is dressed in her best clothes and does not look like someone with advanced cancer. You could have the decency to look ill, I tease her.

The few days turn into eight weeks. Eight weeks of watching Mum get very sick, rally and then get very sick again. She has now been fitted with a catheter and she hates it. At one stage she could not walk but she is now walking again with a frame. The family visit every day never really knowing what to expect. Mum is such a proud lady and on one of her really bad days she banned my sister and I from attending, because she didn't want us to see her so sick. My sister had to sneak in when no one was looking and tell her not to be so silly. Mums' spirit was lifted by a visit from Monty, he was on his best behaviour and lay next to Mum's feet. Mum felt safe at the hospice, she does not want to leave, but we tell her she cannot stay long term as they need the bed for other patients.

I am secretly terrified, how will we cope at home? Mum's granny flat is on the second floor, her mobility is not great, and she will become a prisoner in her own house. I am concerned about the daily nurse visits, we have a dog, some nurses are afraid of dogs. I no longer know how to manage Mum's drugs, she has them through a driver in her arm. What about night time? How can I look after her all through the night? I am desperate for a solution.

Time is running out for Mum at the Hospice and as a last resort my sister and I visit a local nursing home. It looks like a hotel and we are both impressed. It is in walking distance of home so hopefully I can push Mum home in the wheel chair each day and she will have the night care required.

It is really hard telling Mum what we have planned; we feel like we are abandoning her. Mum is assessed and deemed well enough to stay at this nursing home. It is all happening very quickly and before we know it, she is being discharged from the hospice and arriving at her 'temporary' home at the nursing home.

I watch her being put in the ambulance and drive on ahead to meet her at the home. Mum is able to walk into the home and seems quite happy to be there. She has her tea and then my sister and I leave about 9.00pm in the evening, Mum seems tired. We put her to bed and tell the on-duty staff to ring us if Mum needs us, we are very close and will come immediately.

We leave her with very mixed feelings.

We receive no phone calls and presume all is well. I actually drive past the home to get to work in Stratford. I debate with myself, should I go in and see her? I decide that she is probably having breakfast and getting to know the other residents - no I will leave her to settle in.

At lunch time I receive a call from my sister. She has arrived at the home to be told Mum has been very ill in the night, a doctor has been called. My stomach somersaults. Why had they not called? My sister tells me that she will keep me updated when the doctor arrives. She says Mum is sleeping.

I feel awful, she must have been really scared being in a strange place on her own. I am not happy and intend having a serious talk to the staff when I get there. The doctor arrives mid-afternoon and Tina is told that Mum has an infection and some antibiotics are prescribed. Mum still hasn't woken. She shows the doctor a picture of Mum the day before when she arrived, it looks like a different person. He says that infection can take hold quickly. I am due to have acupuncture on my shoulder, the only thing that seems to help the pain at the moment. Tina tells me to go and she will stay with Mum. I call Father Frank and tell him that I am worried about Mum. He is clearly shocked because he only saw her yesterday at the hospice and she looked fine. He tells me to keep him informed.

Father Frank obviously has second thoughts and goes straight to the home. He is horrified at what he sees, he tells Tina he thinks Mum is dying. Phil drives me to the home and as I walk up the corridor, I can hear a horrendous noise, it is Mum trying to breath. Tina is in bits and does not know what to do. There is just one agency nurse on duty who cannot be found anywhere. When I do find her, she tries to tell me that Mum has "just a chest infection". I am not a nurse, but I know my Mum is in a lot of distress and she is dying. I tell her to call an ambulance or I will. She reluctantly calls an ambulance.

The ambulance arrives, and the nurse is immediately talking about Mum's DNR (do not resuscitate) I am livid, I had sat with Mum, in her own home and had helped to persuade her to sign this. I feel like she has signed a death warrant. I take over and explain to the ambulance men that Mum has terminal cancer and had come from an eight week stay in a hospice, she had only been here overnight, and this is the state she is in. I understand what a DNR is, but surely it is not in place to let someone die gasping for breath and in distress. The ambulance men get into action at once. They ask where the oxygen is in the home and why Mum is not on it. Apparently, they are not licensed to keep it! Mum is hooked up to an oxygen mask and I am told that without the oxygen she would be dead in fifteen minutes. They confirm that Mum has sepsis and is dying. They will need to transport her to hospital. I am devastated, after all the planning with the hospice and the Macmillan nurses, Mum is going to die in the corridor of a busy hospital on a Friday night.

I ask the ambulance men if they can wait whilst I ring the Hospice. I know this is a long shot, but I need to try. I still have the direct number to the nursing station at the hospice in my phone. I ring, and it is answered by one of the nurses who had looked after Mum. I tell him what has happened, and I beg him to take her back, to let her die at the hospice. He tells me this is impossible because it is late and there is no doctor to admit her. So, all the planning doesn't matter, all the weeks she has attended and talked about her death, she told you the last place she wanted to be was in hospital. He is silent for a moment and then tells me he will try his best. He will call me back.

I tell the ambulance men what has happened and apologise for keeping them waiting. I know their time is precious. They reassure me that they would rather be taking care of Mum than picking up some drunk who has fallen over. The phone rings and there is a doctor from the hospice on the line, she asks to speak to the ambulance men. I pass the phone over and cross my fingers. After a few minutes the ambulance man gives me the thumbs up. They have a bed and the doctor will meet us at the hospice to admit Mum. They tell Tina and I that Mum may die on route. We are willing to take the risk. The only problem is that they are from Coventry and the hospice is in Solihull. They are not supposed to travel to Solihull, but they are not prepared to wait for another ambulance from Solihull to be called. They have to switch off their navigation system and I will need to direct. Mum is wheeled into the ambulance with Tina holding her hand. I climb in the front. Anthony is driving behind. The siren is switched on and we are off. The ambulance moves quickly, and I feel like I am in some sort of movie!

We arrive at the hospice and are met by the wonderful doctor who has come back to work on a Friday night. It is weird, but it feels like Mum is home. The ambulance crew disappear with Mum and the doctor and we wait anxiously whilst she is assessed and readmitted. The doctor is gentle and kind, she tells us that Mum is back in her old room. She says she does not expect Mum to last the night, but they will check on her. I ask if she will wake up and the doctor says that it is very unlikely as her lungs are flooded from the lack of oxygen. She assures us she is peaceful.

Anthony says his goodbyes to Nan and we tell him to go home. Tina and I settle each side of Mum's bed. We will never leave her again!

Mum is visibly calmer. Throughout the night she is checked regularly, and the nurse makes the decision to move the oxygen mask. Mum is breathing on her own, she is calm, like a sleeping baby.

Daylight appears and at 7.00am we decide to ring the family, Mum has made it through the night, but she is dying. Les, Mum's brother arrives first. He and his wife Pat spend some time talking to Mum and saying goodbye. Tina and I take the time to freshen up. It is now about 11.00am in the morning and the grandchildren arrive on mass. They all look sad. We tell them to come in and talk to Nan. It is bizarre, Beth takes Nan's hand and says hello. From nowhere, Mum opens her eyes and says "hello" back. We are astounded, Mum has woken. I run off to get a nurse. Mum is ushering Tina over and thankfully Tina can help. The nurse at the home had taken Mum's false teeth out. No-one had ever seen Mum without her teeth, she is not happy. Thankfully Tina has her teeth in her handbag! She proceeds to wash them and puts them back in Mums mouth. Our Mum is back.

The nurses come in and they assess Mum again, she is gasping for a cup of tea. The nurses are not sure whether she will be able to swallow it, but they say she can have one. Mum has no memory of the previous night or the night in the home where she got ill. Probably a blessing in disguise. This is something that we will never know. She is safe now.

The doctor talks to us and explains that although Mum has woken, her condition can only get worse. Her lungs are flooded, and she cannot recover from this. They will make her as comfortable as they can. We are very, very grateful for this and for getting the chance to say goodbye properly.

As a family, we surround Mum with love and she is never alone. Tina and I stay and sleep at the hospice. Mum's brother Les returns and makes Mum laugh by saying he has already spent half an hour with her saying goodbye and sloppy things and he won't say them again. But he is grateful to say goodbye properly. Father Frank comes in every day and prays with Mum. Our dog Monty has even been in to say goodbye!

Almost a week has gone by. The strangest week in my life staying at a hospice. Mum said her last words on Wednesday and she is now completely medicated. It is very distressing to watch her organs close down one by one. She no longer looks like Mum. She still has her hair and we comb it daily. She still has her teeth, but her face has become so thin that I am amazed they are staying put.

It is now Friday and the weather has turned outside, it has been hot all week and we have taken it in turns to sit in the lovely gardens. It is now pouring down with rain. We have been in the Hospice a whole week. We had a stressful night because the clock on the wall went mad and started whizzing around for no reason and then the soap dispenser on the wall started to dispense soap. We did not know what was going on. Tina went in search of a nurse who told us not to worry it was something to do with batteries. We are not convinced.

One minute I am urging Mum to stop breathing the next I am urging her to breathe. This is horrible. I tell Oliver and Anthony not to come and see Nan today, they have said their goodbyes every day this week and Mum would not want them seeing her like this.

My sister and I have a bit of a disagreement, she tells me that her children are on the way. I am not happy and insist Mum would hate people seeing her like this, plus the weather is really bad and Tom has only just learnt how to drive.

Something weird happens then. Phil calls me to say he was on his way home from work when suddenly he decided to change his route. He came a completely different way only to see Tom's car stuck in the middle of a busy roundabout. The car is stationary, and he can see all of Tina's grownup children looking terrified in the car. Phil drives back around the island again and stops his van behind Tom's car preventing any other car hitting it. He gets the girls in the van and Tom explains that the car went into a spin and will now not start. Phil manages to restart the car and tells Tom to drive behind the van and follow him home.

Meanwhile at the Hospice, Mum needs to be freshened up and we are asked to wait outside. We pace around wondering how much more we can take. The door suddenly opens, and the nurses appear from the room. Tears are in their eyes and they tell us Mum has gone!

I throw my arms around the nurses and say, "thank goodness". I was right, Mum wanted her privacy, she had always been so dignified. She had not died alone, she had died with the nurse's present. Secretly, I had been terrified of witnessing the end and she had not let that happen.

I am really not sure how I got through the week, but I did. It is not easy saying goodbye, I thank my hidden strength once more. Where would I be without it?

My emotions are all over the place. I am relieved that Mum is out of pain. But this doesn't stop my pain of not having her with me. I throw all my attention to arranging Mum's Celebration of life. Ben is flying back from America to do the eulogy and I am planning the hymns and readings. In fact, I have become such a dab hand at it, the whole service is planned. Father Frank is most impressed.

The church is full for the funeral. Phil, Anthony, Oliver and Tom are pallbearers. Nan would have been so proud of her grandsons. It is a lovely personal mass with the boys doing the readings. I nearly leap from my seat as Anthony visibly stumbles over his words overcome with sadness. It is only for a moment and he continues the reading without issue, Nan has been a big part of his life for twenty-eight years, it is understandable that he will miss her terribly. Oliver does the second reading and I am grateful that he seems fine. Nan is buried close to Tony at Berkswell Churchyard, it is a picture postcard setting and it feels right.

The wake afterwards is well attended and very much a celebration of the life of such a wonderful lady. We are at the same hotel where we held her eightieth birthday party with many of the same people in attendance. I forget to eat and have one glass of wine too many resulting in me having to go to bed early. I am sick and crying, I want my Mum! I can hear Mum's voice in my head saying, "this is self-inflicted Tracey, you should know better." Phil gives me some headache pills and tells me to sleep, "you did her proud".

I return to work and plan a holiday with Lesley and Ray at their house in Spain, they are always there when I need to lick my wounds!

Sadly, this is not the only bad news I have to deal with. Monty has not been himself lately and Phil and I take him to the vets. The vet seems pleased with Monty as he weighs him on the scales. He is pleased because Monty has lost weight. Monty has not been on a diet! The vet proceeds to examine him and his face drops. He looks at us and tells us the news that Monty has cancer. I immediately burst into tears and leave the room. Phil explains to the vet that I have just lost my Mum to cancer and that this will hit me hard. The vet sends us home with some medication which will help Monty. He cannot be cured but the tablets will manage the illness for a little while.

I tell Phil I am cancelling my trip to Spain and he says no, he tells me I need the holiday and that he will stay at home with Monty. He will also get Mum's flat emptied whilst I am away.

I go to Spain and Tina takes Phil's place and for once I do not argue. I need the break and I know it. Phil gives me daily updates on Monty who is doing well. Lesley and Ray make sure we have a nice relaxing week in the sun. When I get home, I am relieved to see that Monty seems well. Mum's flat is now empty and has been redecorated. I did not want it to become a shrine.

I return from work on Wednesday to discover Monty is poorly, he has been very sick. I call Phil and we get him to the vets. Monty picks up at the Vets and he gives him an anti-sickness injection and we bring him home. We know by the time we are home that it was a mistake, Monty is not in a good way. Too late, the Vets have now closed. Monty wants to stay in the garden and we manage to bring him in and we sleep downstairs with him. At first light, we let him back into the garden. He is just lying on the grass. At eight o'clock, Phil goes to the Vets and I stay with Monty. Phil comes back with the vet and we know that the time has come to let Monty go.

It is very quick and peaceful. Phil held him whilst the Vet injects him. He has gone. Tina arrives and kisses him goodbye. We are all distraught, but we know it was the right thing to do. Phil proceeds to dig the biggest hole in the garden and Monty is laid to rest - I spend the whole day crying.

Chapter 14
My Way Forward

I feel at an all-time low. Anthony is working away, Oliver is at University, Mum is gone, and Monty is gone!

I am due to attend my first Women of the Year Awards and luncheon as a guest of Ladies First. Ladies First Professional Development is a networking group I joined earlier in the year. I have enjoyed the meetings that I have attended but they have been few and far between due to Mum's illness. The ticket for this event has cost eighty-five pounds and it seems a huge waste of money if I don't go.

My mind made up, I book a taxi to the venue. The taxi driver has been to the house many times before and immediately asks where the big dog is? He is really apologetic when I explain that he died yesterday. He tries to make small talk and then asks, "how's your Mum?" The look on his face when I tell him that she died six weeks ago! He remains silent for the rest of the journey, his day ruined! For some strange reason I find the incident funny and it feels good to smile.

My mood starts to lift as I join the six hundred plus ladies arriving for the lunch. The noise of laughter and chattering females is infectious, and the glass of champagne soon relaxes me. I forget my troubles for a time whilst wondering through the Convent Garden style shopping area and join up with my fellow table guests. Two of them immediately say they are sorry for my loss and are really glad I decided to come - I am glad too.

We move into the dining area and I am overwhelmed by the atmosphere. It is my introduction to inspirational women and women in business. It is also the first time I meet Pauline Edden one of the Directors of Woman of the Year. The overwhelming support of women supporting each other is incredible. This is definitely a world I want to be part of.

Feeling more uplifted about my future, I can stand the empty house no longer; I need a distraction. I need a puppy. Poor Phil does not know what has hit him, he arrives home from work and he is informed that we are going to get a puppy - NOW. We welcome Maximus, the eight-week-old golden Labrador into our family and chaos commences!

In December, just two months after my Women of the Year experience I am delighted to get the chance to take over Ladies First. The ladies that currently own the business are both getting married next year and no longer have the time to give to the business. Yet again timing is everything.

This is something I really want to do, but not on my own. During a facial with my long-time friend and beautician Julie Richards, I tell her all about the offer and I am delighted when she jumps at the chance to be my new business partner in Ladies First. Neither of us know a lot about networking but we are happy to learn.

Agreements signed, we plan our re-launch at Warwick Castle with the very inspirational Joanne Malin as host. What a venue, the evening is a sell out and portrays the future look for Ladies First. Our motto, "the three I's, to inform, introduce and inspire."

Our plan is to offer a support network to all women, whether they are in employment, run their own business, work from home or who are still in education. We are planning alternative breakfast and lunch meetings at impressive venues with informative and inspirational speakers.

Only a month after the launch I have surgery on my shoulder, after five year's I am hopeful that this might ease my long-term problems following my accident in 2013. I have never had surgery and it is a shock to the system. Six weeks of intensive physio and not driving is frustrating but necessary, I only hope it is worth it.

Our first big achievement is to run our own Business/Inspirational Awards in October 2017, just seven months after our launch. As an event planner, this is one of the hardest events I have ever put together. Once the nominations are in and the candidates interviewed, the fun begins. It is so rewarding seeing all the excitement amongst the finalists, in our book they are all winners and are all given a free ticket to the dinner.

The best part for me is to see the young achievers and inspirational young achievers, our future. It is so important to give the youngsters an opportunity to see into the business world and open doors to their future.

BBC's Coventry & Warwickshire, Journalist and Reporter, Trisha Adudu hosts our event, with keynote speakers Dame Caroline Spelman and Reporter Joanna Tidman. The evening is filled with laughter and tears. An evening to be remembered by all involved thanks to our amazing sponsor, Janine Edwards Wealth Management, another incredible woman. It was particularly special to be supported by Tony's brother David McAtamney, sponsoring an award through his new up and coming business Stadium TM, Tony would have been so impressed.

In March 2018, I am very excited to be invited as a guest of Pauline Edden to the launch of Woman of the Year 2018 at the House of Lords. This is like a dream come true for me, to meet such amazing ladies. It is also particularly special as this is where I first got my vision into supporting and working alongside other women. Ladies First has come a long way in the past year and I do not want to sit still, my enthusiasm is stronger than ever.

Throughout the year Ladies First has also been in action - fundraising. When we launched the business, we pledged to raise £7321, the amount required to run Marie Curie Hospice in Solihull for a day. We have finally achieved this at a Fashion Show and our day has been confirmed as

19th August 2018, in memory of my Mum, Shirley Thomas and on the second anniversary of her death.

In April 2018, we launch our WOW group, aptly named by my son Anthony, Women of Wisdom. This is all under the same umbrella as Ladies First, but it is aimed to attract ladies who perhaps are coming to the end of their careers, ladies who still enjoy the speakers and lunches but are not necessarily looking for networking for business. It is also a great group of ladies to share their experiences with those just starting out. This is the event where I make my first real speech, it is based on the fact that I believe everyone in the room has their own story and so I tell my story!

From this, I have met some amazing ladies who have supported and nurtured me into writing my story. The lovely, Samantha Houghton, who has been by my side all the way offering support and giving me the confidence to put pen to paper. She said it would help to heal the trauma of Tony's sudden death, now fourteen years ago, the trauma of watching my Mum die of cancer and explain the journey of where I am today; it has. Thank you, Sam.

I am also privileged to be invited to be part of Susie Mackie's Women of Spirt. I'll have a portrait taken, and a short version of my memoir will be completed, to be part of the chapter 'Death Does Not Define Me'. What a whirlwind.

Chapter 15
Why Now?

2018/19 are special years for me in so many ways. Telling my story has opened so many boxes which I had closed over the years. I have shed tears now which I did not give myself permission to do when Tony died.

If anyone asks me, what is the worst thing you have ever had to do in your life? The answer is simple - to tell a seven-year-old that his Daddy has died and is not coming home.

My boys were aged fifteen and seven at the time of Tony's death. Nothing can prepare you as a mother, father or guardian on how to cope with death in a family, especially sudden death.

I was lucky in some ways because Tony's strong faith had been passed on through him to the boys. They both attended church schools and were given ongoing spiritual support, but it also gave me a means to try and make some sense of the situation, especially when telling Oliver.

Overnight I lost my husband, father to my children, best friend and soulmate. The sense of loss and despair was overwhelming. The feeling of emptiness which hurts so much that your lungs constrict and make the ability to think and breathe seem impossible. For me, Tony's death was also very public. It made front page news in the Coventry Evening Telegraph and I felt like I was in a gold fish bowl with everyone looking in.

Once I found the strength to breathe again, gradually, I was able to think and make decisions, decisions that I had never dreamed I would have to make, emotional decisions, legal decisions, business decisions and financial decisions none of which I had been prepared to do. The main instinct of all was to protect my boys, the rest just followed.

I am not an author or writer of any kind. The story I have told is a diary of events that changed my life forever, in my own words and from the heart. It is a journey of how I have got to where I am today and explains who I have become. I am quite certain if I met Tony again today, he would not recognise me.

I am not special or inspirational, I am a Mother who would move heaven and earth to protect her family. I found a hidden strength which I didn't know existed within me and my greatest achievement in life has been raising my boys and seeing them grow into the wonderful young men they have become.

Anthony has just turned thirty and has recently got engaged to Tammie, his girlfriend of five years. Tammie is Australian and has just completed a Chemistry PHD at Warwick University. Anthony is extremely successful at his job and is now happy in love.

Oliver is twenty-one and has just graduated with a 2.1 in Politics & International Relations at the University of Nottingham, he has the world at his feet.

Fourteen years ago, the worry of how they would cope without their Father was paramount. It wasn't easy as they are both dyslexic making school an extra challenge. But they rose to each and every challenge presented to them both emotionally and academically - I couldn't be prouder.

I consider myself very fortunate, things could have turned out very different for us all without the amazing people in my life.

Firstly, my Mum. I had an incredible Mother, and Nan to the boys. She was the most inspirational woman I have ever met. The last part of my story talks about losing her, the trauma and pain of watching someone you love slowly dying is unbearable, but yet again it is incredible where you gain the strength, courage and confidence to deal with the things you never imagine you could do.

My Mum, sister and my friends have always been there for me. They supported me through the bad times and held my hand when things seemed impossible. Godparents, Alex and Fiona Ambrosioni, Christina and Brian Richards and Alison McDowall have been supportive then and now in every sense of the word, supporting Anthony and Oliver with endless love and guidance.

My step children, Helen, Victoria and Gerard, Tony would now have been the proud Granddad of four grandchildren; Indira, Xavier, Juniper and Teddy. Our special bond remains stronger than ever.

I know the massive impact Tony's death had on so many of our friends and family. Many are still by my side today and remember the night of his death as if it was yesterday. They shared the pain of having to tell the children and watching how they reacted at the time and over the years.

Phil came into my life at the right time and has provided Oliver with the grounding and male bonding he, in particular, missed so much when losing his Dad. He has provided us all with the love and support needed, especially through Mum's illness.

My faith has been vital to me. I cannot say that I have any great understanding or reasoning of religion or the Catholic Church, but I do know it has comforted me in my time of need. Quite often when things have seemed hopeless, I have just sat quietly in church and prayed for answers to my problems and the answers have come!

Fundraising has always played a huge part in my life. I have always got a real buzz from giving back especially to charities who have touched my life in some way. Fundraising has led me to where I am today. My work with Ladies First is both fulfilling and rewarding, every day the people I meet inspire me, they all have their own story to tell, many conquering adversities to find their own path to success and happiness.

As for me, the person I have become is enthusiastic, positive, optimistic and determined but on the down side I know that I always have to feel in control. I don't share my problems and I make my own decisions, making me not the easiest person to live with! I know that you cannot control all the events which happen to you in life, but you can control how you deal with them.

In June 2019 we will be travelling to Portugal to join the Law Society Golf Club to present the Tony McAtamney Cup, it will be fifteen years since his sudden death. Time does heal the pain, but the memories are for keeps, no one can take them away.

I sincerely hope that reading my story will help anyone dealing with bereavement to show them that there is light at the end of every tunnel. The greatest power in my life has been my hidden strength, this lives within each and every one of us and only shows itself in times of desperation and when our loved ones need us to be strong.

About the Book

All proceeds from the sale of my book will go towards my new project, The McAtamney Foundation.

The McAtamney Foundation will provide children and young adults with support through bereavement in the following ways:

- By providing free Memory Boxes to children and young adults. These will be given following death or in the case of illness, will be provided for loved ones to work on together prior to death.

- Companies will be asked to provide sponsorship, information and items for the Memory Boxes. The Memory Boxes can be ordered online via the website, through Schools, Doctors and Hospitals.

- Counselling will be found and provided for those children in need.

The Tracey McAtamney website will provide relevant and up to date information on the following:

Seminars

- Legal Advice
- Wealth Management Advice
- Benefit Advice
- Help Line

As a parent, the most important thing is the emotional wellbeing of children effected by death. Children have an amazing resilience and the ability to deal with sadness. The not knowing is worse for them, we cannot protect children from sadness but we can share feelings and support them in their sadness.

There is no wrong or right way to deal with bereavement and unfortunately for those left behind heartache and sadness are not the only issues to deal with. It is my vision to provide free memory boxes and to work with other charities to provide support and information. Our seminars will provide a platform for people going through similar situations to share their stories and for them to find answers to all those impossible questions.

www.traceymcatamney.co.uk and my email address is traceymcatamney@btconnect.com

I was only seven when my Father died, and it has been really interesting for me to read my Mum's Memoir. I know this is a story of our lives, but sometimes it feels like it happened to someone else. I know our lives changed in an instant with just one telephone call. I try very hard to remember my Father, I know we were very close. I know that I have blocked certain memories out, but I do remember I hated people being sad, especially my Mother. I remember missing my Father at school events in particular when other children's Dads were present.

There has been a huge gap while growing up, but my Father's memory has always been kept alive. As a family, we often talk about him and some of the funny things he did to make us laugh, especially when we are all together.

I know my Mother had lots of problems to deal with at the time of my Father's death, but they were always kept from me. She always saved the smiles for me.

My Mother has always been there for me, she always encouraged me to make the most of every opportunity and taught me that no matter how bad a situation can seem there is always a light at the end of the tunnel and things will be okay.

I believe the sadness I suffered as a young child has made me stronger. Certainly, it helped me cope with my Nan's terminal illness and her death in the Hospice. It has also given me a special empathy with friends who are coping with bereavement.

I hope my Mother's Memoir can help others going through similar situations. I'm very proud of her!

Oliver

Like most people who have lost a parent or loved one, I can clearly remember the last time I saw them. It was a bright summers morning, my Father was sitting at the kitchen table, a broad-sheet newspaper in hand, having breakfast and chatting merrily to my grandmother. He kissed me goodbye, and I was out the front door with my mother and brother to help at a children's birthday party.

That memory is so vivid for me because, in contrast to when I physically saw my Fathers' body for the final time, it was so utterly devoid of everything that was him, his spirit and love of life, that's what I struggled to recognise.

There is never a good time to lose a parent. However, I consider myself fortunate that it was already a time of change in my life. In the space of six weeks, I lost my Father, I had a new school, a new job and new friends. With so much of the routine of my life changed, I was distracted enough that the full grief and realisation did not crash into me, but rather over the years, drips and drops of it hit me when the absence became almost a presence, birthdays, Christmases, Easter and graduations. The main change for me at these times is that I feel the loss but also the joy and happiness that he would have at those moments.

The one constant, unyielding thread throughout my life has been my mother. Right from my earliest memories, she has been fighting my corner and keeping the world in check. During those dark days and months, she dealt with a situation that was at times farcical in its absurdity. The strength, love, tolerance and depth of character that she displayed has been and continued to be an inspiration to me. I count my mother as the first and main reason I am who I am.

I am pleased she has put pen to paper to express her feelings of loss and her coping mechanism over the years since.

Anthony